Architecture for the future

Architecture for the future

·TERRAIL·

Front cover illustration
Lyons Opera House,
France.
Jean Nouvel.

Frontispiece
Exhibition Hall,
Nagoya, Japan.
Itsuko Hasegawa.

Editors : Jean-Claude Dubost and Jean-François Gonthier
Cover design : Gérard Lo Monaco and Laurent Gudin
Art Director : Bruno Leprince
Editorial Assistant : Claire Néollier
English Text adapted by Peter Snowdon
Typesetting : Graffic, Paris
Origination : Litho Service T. Zamboni, Verona

© ÉDIGROUP/ÉDITIONS TERRAIL, PARIS 2004
25-27, Rue Ginoux - 75015 Paris - France
ISBN: 2-87939-028-1
Printed in France

CONTENTS

PERPETUAL MOTION

Foreword by Olivier Boissière

Prediction is a hazardous exercise. Even H.G.Wells and Aldous Huxley got it wrong. 1984 has come and gone. Big Brother is merely a ghostly memory and we are still waiting for our Brave New World.

It might seem paradoxical, naive, even pretentious to try and assess the future, but there are at least two good reasons for attempting to do so. First of all, architecture is itself an art of the future, a perpetual project whose plans are constantly being redrawn. The second reason is more concrete and more reassuring: architecture is a slow-moving art, closely dependent on economic, political and social factors, and on changing fashions. It is therefore quite legitimate to attempt to decipher premonitory signs, symptoms, and trends in contemporary architectures, from which we might cautiously infer long-term consequences.

Utopia and science fiction share two characteristics. One is a positive ambition to develop a specific vision of the world's and of mankind's future. The other is a propensity to edit out some fundamental aspect of reality, introducing in its place some purely imaginary condition: thus gravity may cease to exist, or the natural rhythm of the seasons come to a halt.

During what has been called its "heroic"[1] period, architecture embraced two overlapping utopias. The first, inspired by a new industrial impetus in the aftermath of the First World War, credited rationalised production with the supernatural power to create an ideal order which would utterly transform society, liberate creative forces, and give birth to a new man. The second – perhaps a mere illusion – was the idea that the architect, whose scope of activity would range from industrial design to town planning (from the dessert spoon to the city), would be the agent of such transformation, a literal *deus ex machina* capable of shaping a destiny for mankind: "Architecture or Revolution" as Le Corbusier ill-advisedly put it. The result was a spate of speeches and manifestos, of movements – De Stijl in the Netherlands, Constructivism in the Soviet Union – and schools, such as the Bauhaus in Weimar, and later Dessau, or the Vkhutmas in Moscow.

Conic intersection
Paris, 1975
Gordon Matta Clark (1943 - 1978)

An architectural intervention on the last 18th-century buildings in an area undergoing redevelopment. Through the cone, the Pompidou Centre, then under construction, was visible from a totally unexpected angle.

1. In general, this period is taken to run between 1910 and 1933. Cf. Peter and Alison Smithson, *The Heroic Period of Modern Architecture*, Thames& Hudson, London, 1981.

The most notorious heralds of this impending golden age were Van Doesburg and El Lissitzky, Walter Gropius and Le Corbusier*. A new vision was taking shape.

Vilém Flusser[2] aptly reminds us that our term "theory" derives from the Greek word for "vision" – *theoria*. A new theory was accordingly elaborated, which sought to do away with the "old architecture" and establish a new framework worthy of democracy triumphant. It aimed to transform both the city and life, freeing the forces of reason to build an ideal world. This universal ambition rapidly veered towards dogmatism. Le Corbusier's 'five points', for instance – free plan, horizontal strip windows, pilotis, roof-gardens, and free, non-load-bearing facades – were they not simply intended to replace the tenets of 19th-century treatises? Argument still rages, not as to their relative validity but as to their original intent: were such theoretical principles *constructional* or *aesthetic*? In 1932, the Americans Philip Johnson and Henry-Russell Hitchcock (the dandy and the critic) offered their response and sounded the knell of utopia by calling their exhibition at the New York Museum of Modern Art, "The International Style". When all was said and done, was it merely a question of style? Messianic modern architecture had had its day. The barque of love had foundered on the rocks of everyday life. Then came the invasion of Poland, Pearl Harbour, Stalingrad, the Holocaust and Hiroshima, the Berlin Wall and Vietnam, the loss of innocence and the fall from grace. The architect had to come to terms with the new world order: he was not to be the demiurge, the catalyst of social change he had dreamed of becoming, but merely an obscure hero with limited responsibilities. Rather than shaping life, he would design its context, giving form – where possible discreetly – to the *genius loci* and to the spirit of the age.

Today, if a utopian yearning still exists, it is a purely regressive phenomenon, represented by those few who still proclaim their nostalgic faith in a society free of concrete and metal, social tension and unemployment.

Within a few decades, both the 20th century and architecture have witnessed the demise of over-arching narratives, all-embracing ideologies and infexible dogmas. In a complex and contradictory world where reality is fragmentary, they have shed their illusions. A single, vast, inoperable theory has been replaced by a galaxy of small, usable, "tool-box"[3] theories tailored to projects limited in time and space. Deprived of a grand scheme, architecture has reappropriated a territory of its own, where the useful and the sublime have, somehoro, been reconciled.

And what of progress? It remains the central preoccupation for a significant number of architects, despite a popularly held view that its effects are highly questionable, if not directly nefarious. And rightly so! The veritable advent of modern architecture was marked by technical innovation – metallic structures, clad in concrete, traversed by lifts. Technology has transformed architecture irreversibly. A list of the milestones in this saga would clearly include Crystal Palace*, Le Baron Jenney's steel-framed building in Chicago[4], the Eiffel Tower, the Flat Iron building in New York, and the now demolished hangar at Orly by Freyssinet. To which might well be added

Objects fused together by heat from the bomb at Hiroshima
1945.

2. Vilém Flusser, philosopher and theoretician, in *World Architecture* n°27, 1993.
3. Michel Foucault and Gilles Deleuze, in *L'Arc*, 1972.
4. *Home Insurance Building*, 1885.

* For names and terms followed by an asterisk, see glossary.

the Crimean War assembly-kit field hospital designed and built by the great engineer Isambard Kingdom Brunel[*] for the intrepid nurse Florence Nightingale, whose component parts were dismantled, recycled and sold off after hostilities had ceased.

It is therefore hardly surprising that architects have been enthralled by the fantasy of technical progress. This century counts a number of brilliant innovators, architects-cum-engineers, and engineers-cum-architects, such as the American Buckminster Fuller, the Frenchman Jean Prouvé, the Italians Morandi and Nervi, the Mexican Felix Candela, and Britain's Ove Arup, Peter Rice and Tony Fitzpatrick[*]. Working alone or in partnership, they explore the limits of constructional technique, constantly on the look-out for new materials, carrying out *ad hoc* transfers of technology from space research or polymer chemistry. They play a vital role in boosting performance levels, lightening structures, and freeing up large, flexible spaces. Champions of constructive truth or willing victims of the machine aesthetic, these technological crusaders might well have pursued low-key, somewhat marginal careers had it not been for the founding of Archigram[*] in the early 1960s. In a short-lived blaze of activity, the effects of which are still felt today, this exhuberent young group of designers introduced an explosive blend of the best in the British engineering tradition with the extravagance of the fashion world, the blare of advertising, and the imminent sexual revolution, propelling architecture into the MacLuhan galaxy. The Pompidou Centre remains the most fully-achieved demonstration of the Archigram approach although it is now quite dated: in today's automated, miniaturised world, this type of technical expressivism is on the wane. A new preoccupation, that of form, is emerging among the high-tech generation. But was the absence of form not already a kind of form in itself?

Victor Hugo had predicted the death of architecture, believing that the spread of the written word would deprive the former of its code-bearing role. Were the late 19th century and the budding industrial revolution the swan song of this art form? Never in its history had architecture experienced such unbridled eclecticism, such a riot of ornamentation. Young, modern architects were nauseated by the turn-of-the-century surfeit of ornate motifs, Viennese frills, and Art Nouveau circumvolutions. The Viennese architect Adolf Loos[*] denounced ornamentation as a crime; sobiety was the order of the day. Armed with the new, definitive conviction that beauty was use, they developed a rigorous rationalism, in which a puritanical respect for geometrical form was barely tempered by a taste for colour, where possible primary. It is to be noted that this approach was the fruit of a dominant, yet by no means exclusive school of thought: the champions of functional architecture like Gropius and Mies Van der Rohe[*], before presiding over the fortunes of the Bauhaus, had been enthusiastic members of the Novembergruppe[*], whose members pusued a highly imaginative and expressionistic style and which survived long after those two masters had made their U-turn. Nor could the use of form by the Russian Constructivists have properly been called ascetic.

The post-war spread of the International Style signalled its decline: the pursuit of "pure" architecture mercilessly exposed mediocrity. Few could match Mies Van der Rohe and mute curtain-wall facades were soon a worn-out cliché. The rehabilitation of form was heralded by Robert Venturi[*].

The Eiffel Tower under construction 1889.

In two seminal works – two "gentle manifestos" – *Complexity and Contradiction in Architecture* and *Learning from Las Vegas*, Venturi revalorized an architecture that was rich, inclusive and "impure", deriving its references both from history and from an emerging, vibrant, popular culture. By pinpointing street life, commercial advertising, and shopping malls as the crucibles of urban vitality, Venturi was, perhaps unwittingly, among those responsible for bringing architecture back down to earth, and for putting an end to the discipline's relative autonomy. Then came the Ronchamp* chapel in the French Jura, which astonished the public (and was a subject of great perplexity for the young James Stirling*). Le Corbusier, apostle of the "machine for living in", author of the "ode to the right angle", had produced this complicated, generous, sensual building, full of folds and curves. Architecture was awakening from a long sleep; it shook itself and, gazing around, realised that the world was changing. It rediscovered its affinities with the visual arts and their evolution over the past half-century. Suprematism, Concrete Art and Expressionism were reappraised. Neo-Dadaism, Pop Art, Minimal and Conceptual Art were embraced. It became clear that an infinite variety of possibilities had replaced monopolistic conformity as the contemporary aesthetic. Technology has removed all barriers. Cultural homogenisation brought about by the free flow of information has paradoxically engendered the assertion of identity and difference. The proliferation of images has invested the semantic field with a new importance, thus proving Victor Hugo wrong, and allowing architecture once more freely to encapsulate the spirit of its time and to embody the *genius loci*. By ignoring geography and pursuing the *tabula rasa* as an obsession, modern architecture had ended up by confusing context and world, nature and public gardens. The energy crisis and a new ecological awareness brought it back down to earth. Think globally, act locally: such is the watchword of a whole generation, one which also ponders the type of relationships it can establish with a natural world that has been profoundly altered by industrial society. A new sensitivity to natural phenomena and the ways in which they can be harnessed by technology is emerging, filtering the heat of the sun and taming the wind, creating a relationship that is at once economical and sensual. Beautiful *and* useful?

"Light is", proclaimed the great American architect Louis Kahn. He had in mind divine, natural light, the distant gleam of the stars. He pretended not to know, or to consider as insignificant, that man in his infinite ingenuity had invented electricity. More than a century after its appearance, electricity continues to fascinate. Produced nowadays from a wide variety of sources, its multi-coloured light pervades our cities and their architecture.

One day in 1925, the Italian physicist and Nobel prize winner, Guglielmo Marconi, transmitted a radio signal from his boat in the Mediterranean that, by a single pulse, flooded the City Hall in Sydney with light. Our late 20th-century architects should spare him a kindly thought. For a handful of them are striving to create just such a miraculous aesthetic, as they explore the fields of electronics and communication, investigate networks and fibre optics, and connect up to video screens and computers. The architecture they hold out as a promise, and of which we have already been offered glimpses, is made of images, swirling clouds, holograms and

Building in the shape of an electric plug
1967.
Gouache.
Claes Oldenburg

insubstantial veils. It is an immaterial architecture, a conjurer's architecture revealing the futility and anxiety of a society in a state of continuous flux.

The texts and images which follow highlight a wide range of questions and possible answers. Through them, a vision of the future is slowly taking shape.

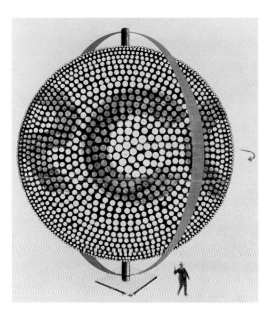

Project for a luminous advertizing sphere 1924.
Herbert Bayer

Project for Peace Pavilion
Universal Exhibition, Paris, 1937.
Laprade and Bazin

1. ATTITUDES

"Not happiness for all, but happiness for each of us".
Boris Vian

The end of our century has been marked by the collapse of ideology and the demise of grand theoretical ambition. Architecture too has had its share of would-be universal principles, of unique and definitive solutions to the fate of humankind, of dogmatic excess. But this is no longer a time for all-embracing manifestos, whose weaknesses are all too quickly exposed by reality.

Faced with a world that is both complex and unpredictable, architectural thinking has become both more modest and more pragmatic. Rather than elaborating grand theories, the emphasis is on foregrounding given situations, small-scale predicaments and specific attitudes. A "soft" approach. The age of proselytism is past. Theory is now the "tool box" of the philosophers Foucault and Deleuze. It is necessarily active, and its activity may be what saves it from delusions of its own importance.

The texts in this section demonstrate the diversity of preoccupations and perspectives that prevails in the profession today. They raise some central questions about architecture, the world, and the relationship between the two: the role of the avant-garde (Peter Cook); the threat to modernity (Daniel Libeskind); the event as the structuring element in the project (Bernard Tschumi); the renewal of the phenomenology of perception (Arakawa and Gins); war as a context for architecture (Lebbeus Woods); and strategies for confronting an elusive reality (François Roche).

This mosaic of reflections represents, of course, only one small part of the wide range of ideas that are at work in architecture today. ∎

Opposite
National Studio for Contemporary Art
Tourcoing, France.
Bernard Tschumi

PETER COOK

London, Great Britain

In optimistic, swinging London, in the early sixties, the emergence of Peter Cook and Archigram* was a revolution of the same order as pop and the miniskirt. Archigram took all the ideas that had been debated throughout the fifties by the Independent Group*, a group combining artists and critics, – took them literally, and tried to give them form, drawing on the conventions of the cartoon strip. Over the space of ten years, Archigram was to invent a hedonistic architectural vision of the future that paid homage to technology, the media and consumer society. In doing so, it determined (particularly in the work of Cedric Price[x]) the archetypes of British high tech.

Since that time, Peter Cook has continued to create his own architecture, based on flexible programmes and an ecological awareness. Visually, his work has become more gentle and more expressive, as it has made space for nature and for colour.

Office Building
Hamburg, Germany.

Notes on an Avant-Garde Architecture
Essay

At this moment in history we are supposed to be wary of the role of the avant-garde, perhaps because it was predominant in the early part of the century and therefore at the wrong time for us in terms of acceptable historical cycles, or perhaps because it threatens the neat structure of architectural categorization by its maverick patterns of play.

The avant-garde often set itself against the procedures of the day, as well as its icons. At its best, however, it attempted to explode the entire system of relationships: dismantling the language of criticism, the tonal scale, the frame, or the medium of transmission while affronting the eye, mind, or ear with more than a mere alternative. Perhaps the major weakness of much architectural avant-gardism is its habit of integrating itself back into the mainstream at too early a point. While this is understandable in that architecture is a social and useful art, it is puzzling in light of the plethora of drawn architectural statements of the last few years. Even without being partisan as to style or content, one can say that very few architectural projects attend to the question of fundamental composition or the aesthetics of the chain of events, although literature, music, and dance have been involved in just such a revolution within the same period. Daniel Libeskind, in his ability to sum up gambits that are clearly related to both mathematics and music, Coop Himmelblau in their consistent attempt to "dart" across all the carefully documented niceties of task, place, and space by capturing the instantaneous, the first gesture – each in their own way displays a fearlessness and, more significantly, a wish to bypass (or is it reinvent?) the tyranny of additive and circumstantial thinking in architecture. In this sense, they are surely in the tradition of the best of the avant-garde. We can examine their work on the level of a captured dynamic, whether or not the actual artefacts have a symbolic dynamic. Essentially, they contribute to the re-creation of the culture of architecture by concentrating upon its process.

Sudden lurches of architectural magic do occur in a particular place, and the spirit of the individuals concerned is bound up with their view of themselves in that place and of that place. In the nineteenth century we could find great cities of action - Glasgow, Buffalo, Berlin - where architecture could run along beside the audacities and aspirations of the city and therefore include a disproportionately large quantity of inventive (and opportunistic) building. Other cities, emerging as replacements of Vienna, Rome, or St. Petersburg, craved cultural recognition. Sometimes they strove to define sophistication by adopting a high style, as in the case of Brussels and Art Nouveau. In the twentieth century it has become a more furious and less monumental trade, one of money, power, and influence, with the architecturally interesting cities distributed unevenly. Any examination of these cities has to take into account the particular city's aspirations, its patronage structure and how that may be manifested, and – to use that word again – its "spirit."

The greatest cities do not fit comfortably into this scheme. New York is too supportive of the idea of measurable (and provable) success to easily handle the new at the point of pain, preferring to wait until creative clones have been bred. Paris is too much in love with the memory of its position as the cradle of the artistic avant-garde to be able to do more than host visiting virtuosi – hence the programme of Grands Projets. (It remains to be seen whether these will act as a catalyst for any creative architectural life within the Paris studios themselves.) At the same time, London is experiencing one of its periodic fits of philistinism, encouraged by the Prince of Wales; any evidence of strange or inventive work is viewed as part of the tradition of English eccentricity and therefore amusing but harmless (meaning, of course, not worth bothering about).

Yet such cities possess more than their fair share of influence. Air travel and the accumulation of academies, publishing houses, and world-networked professionals feed the insidious (though creative) institution of architectural chitchat. This in itself becomes a useful structure within which to shock, amaze, and tantalize, generating a vicious competitiveness that favours the energetic and ambitious while forcing a certain conformity on potentially original work.

What is important in determining the essential difference between most "spirited" architecture and work that has coarsely been termed "post-modern", is the question of space, physical ambition, and rhetoric. The post-modern condition most often depends on figuration, profile, automation, and a com-positional manner more akin to graphic design than to three-dimensional design. What links the opportunistic design of the nineteenth century, modernism and the new explosive architecture lies outside these constraints. The new work also does not need quotation to gain our interest. In some senses it is more primeval, inherently tantalized by the challenge of capturing space and welding substance; it reminds one of the effort involved and then revels in some of the distortions and diversions possible along the way. The fascination, for instance, that Toyo Ito and Itsuko Hasegawa have with layering

Way Out West
Berlin, Germany.
Elevation from the square.

semi-transparent skins and then drawing analogies between them and the natural phenomena of clouds or forests remains a primeval wish to be associated with the basic observable elements of nature.

The distance of their city, Tokyo, from the rest of the world in which twentieth-century architecture is discussed and exchanged forces a self-consciousness that manifests itself in two ways. The first is the awareness of layers and layers of accumulated sophistication that involve craft, myth, placement, illusion, and manners. The other is a delight in the newness and the sheer availability of the fruits of the twentieth century. Hasegawa can only have experienced joy in landing large domes and metallic hills and forests in a dreary part of Tokyo's outer suburbia, in the same way that Masaharu Takasaki must have revelled in placing his egg-like form and its attendant antennae into the bourgeois area of Shinjuku in Tokyo. Of course, we can soften the argument by remembering that Tokyo is essentially a city of bricolage, where there are frequent shifts of reference, grain, intensity, and substance. Nonetheless, it remains the most potentially ripe ground for new and experimental architecture.

In the ostensibly different conditions of Los Angeles, the most catalytic factor remains that of the place itself as if the threat of descent into the sea and the avoidance of acknowledging a centre were a mandate for anti-architecture. The exaggerated beach town has created gems and Frank Gehry has inherited the vigour with which West Coast artists have reacted to the special mixture of light and landscape, escapism and invention. He is a cultural figure, raising the status of building in the city; a coercive figure, creating a virtual school; and an ambassador for the West Coast, working by invitation and commission across the coast and deep into Europe.

As the mode of controlled bricolage is transferred to other talent, we can ask what is especially powerful about the Angelino model. Surely it is that essentially twentieth-century quality of equal value and equal acquisition. The plethora of forms and materials that can be incorporated into buildings in that city seems to force architects to really think hard. No longer can they fall back on the dictates of manners of the street, the cornice line, or the consistency of infill. Architects as different as Morphosis and Aks Run succeed in establishing new and original values as well as forms for the relaxed city.

Equally inventive in its use of regional inspirations – and in progression beyond them – is the recent architecture of Spain where present practitioners have created a sophisticated architectural culture in Barcelona that embraces Oscar Tusquets at its more theatrical extreme and Piñón and Viaplana at its more contemplative. Their offspring, Carme Pinós and Enric Miralles do, however, draw from far more than a regional set of influences. The atmosphere of Barcelona is by nature tough and critical.

It remains to be seen how the global discussion of values and forms will affect that country, which is now politically and economically in a mood for expansion. In terms of the architectural mainstream, it is possible to compare Spain with Holland. In both there is a greater percentage of good architects than in other European countries, but is there a genuinely new spirit?

It may well be that the architectural initiative of the next twenty years will come from a country or a city that has hitherto been considered on the periphery. We need only consider the important roles played by Sweden in the 1940s, Brazil in the 1950s, and Spain at this moment, and then contemplate their previous obscurity. Perhaps the hotbed of a "post-tech" architecture will

Way Out West Berlin
Berlin, Germany.
Detail of the section.

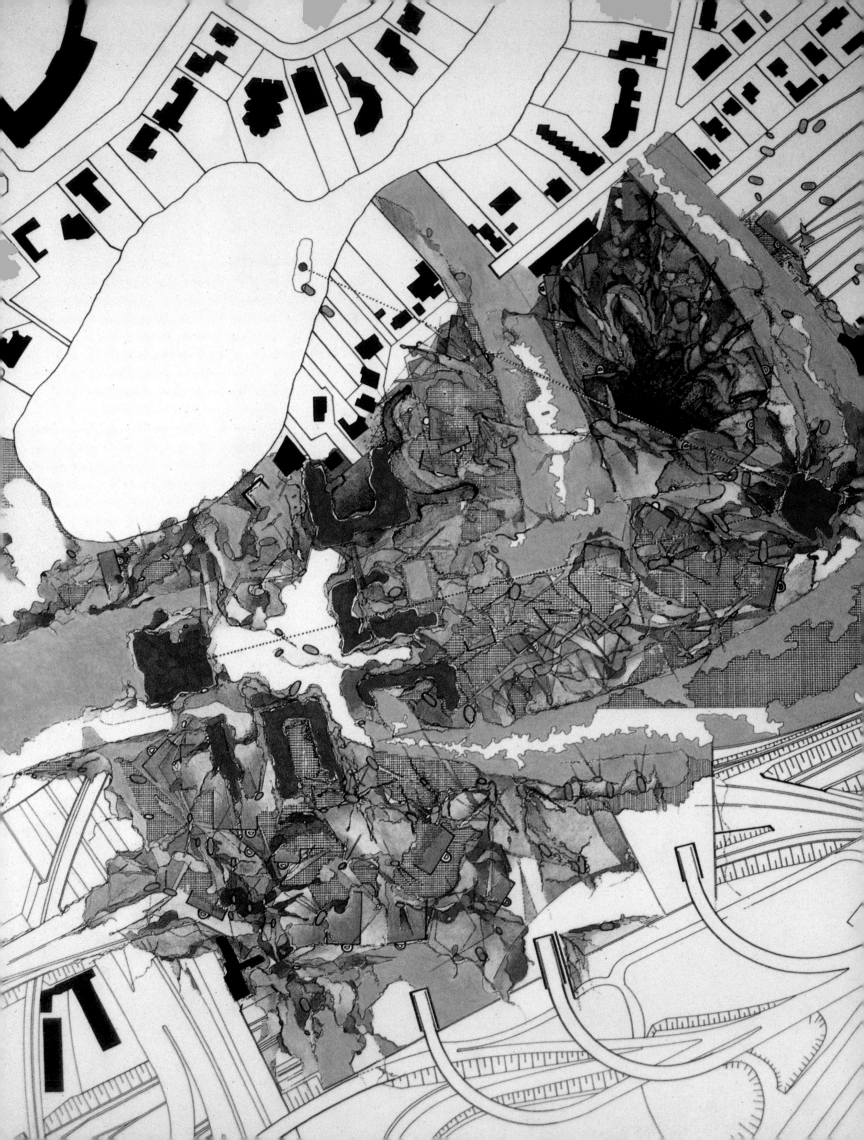

be Australia (with its remarkably inventive band of architects, who seem to pick up on the technical tradition of metal buildings in the Australian outback with increasing sophistication), or perhaps the Czech Republic or Hungary (with their sophisticated European background that has been wound up like an unused spring), or Canada. The candidate for such a role will most likely be "first-world," since highly developed buildings are expensive.

Opposite
Way Out West
Berlin, Germany.
Location plan.

Loft
Section

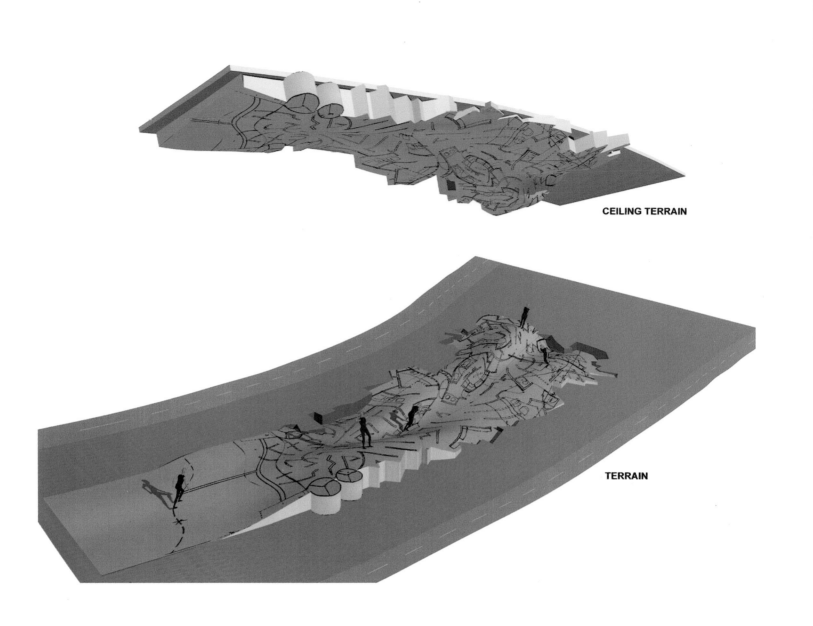

CEILING TERRAIN

TERRAIN

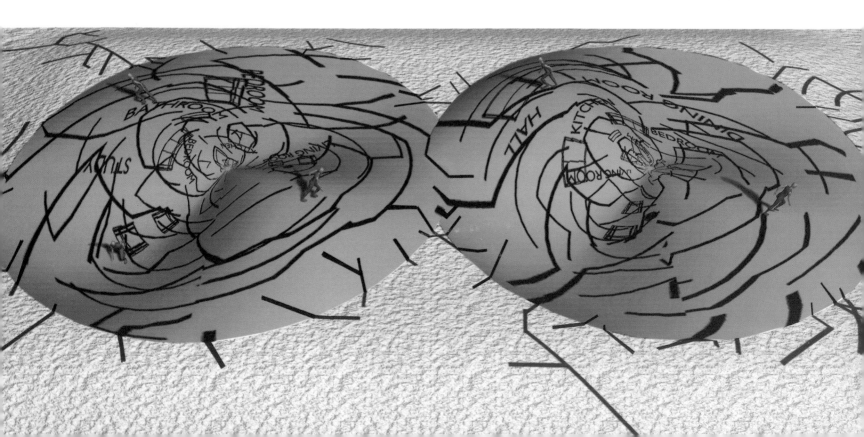

ARAKAWA AND MADELINE GINS

New York, USA

Time was the major preoccupation of Arakawa's work as a painter in the 1960s. Today, the installations he produces in collaboration with Madeline Gins are ways of exploring both philosophical and aesthetic issues. The standard conditions of perception are overturned by poetically explosive systems which seek to transcend the categories of space, the material and the immaterial, the sensorial and the non-sensorial, so as to defeat time through the invention of a reversible destiny.

Reversible Destiny Houses

The first Reversible Destiny House and the Reversible Destiny Office are located at Gifu in Japan. A provisional agreement has been reached for the construction of Reversible Destiny Middle-Income Housing.

- It may take a few hours to go from the living room to the kitchen.
- Terrain predominates over plan.
- The only destiny worth talking about is a reversible one.
- Houses will consist primarily of entrances.
- Walls will be entered.

Complex conversations will be carried on between the body and the terrain. It will be a moot point from moment to moment which of them will take the lead.

- The house will be valued for the instability it provides.
- Labyrinth and house will be cross-bred.
- Every labyrinth will have its centre removed and the frustrations that it offers re-worked.
- Distinctly different re-worked labyrinths (or collections of labyrinth-derived patterns of wall segments) will be used one above the other in contradistinction to one another.
- It will not be possible to take an unambiguous step.
- An area with a ten-foot ceiling height may contain from two to nine distinctly different layers of labyrinth-derived segmenting.
- A kitchen may be an exact replica of the garden it faces.
- There will be parts of the kitchen or living room that will reappear in the bedroom and in the bathroom.
- Some rooms will make reappearances but with oppositely pitched terrains.
- Nothing will be allowed to stand on its own.
- There will be a superabundance of references, a surfeit of landing sites.
- The underside of things will always be ready at hand.

Left
Reversible Destiny Housing

Above
Ceiling terrain and terrain.
Below
Model.

21

– Whenever possible the rising of structures up off the ground will be taken step (or, rather, less-than-step) by step so as not to have perception led by "the abrupt."

– Use and convenience will be re-invented.

– It may take several days to find everywhere in the house that the dining room is.

– The modern will become rococo along specific lines and volumes for parsing experience.

– Communal settings will provide double and triple horizons.

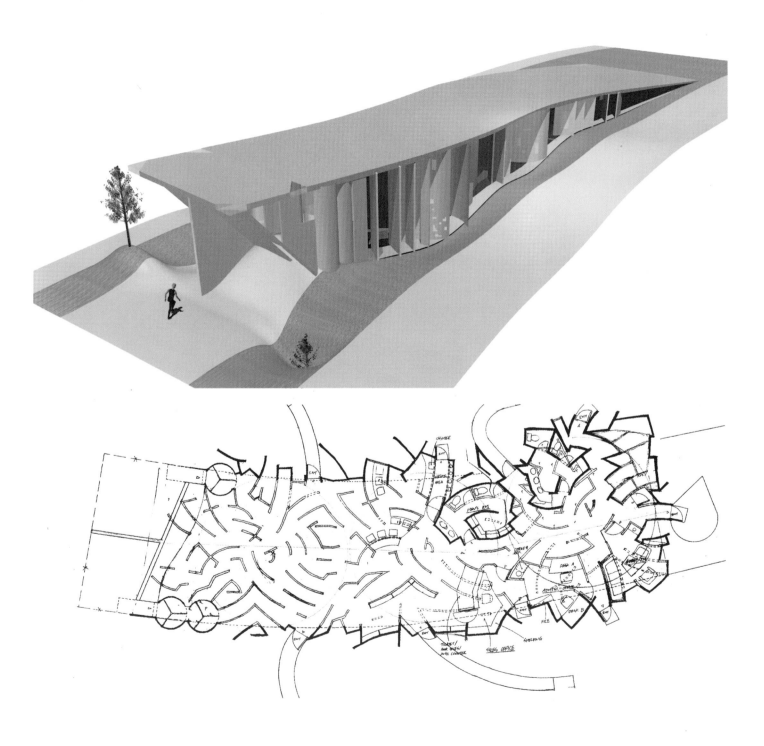

– Liverpool and Antarctica will be joined and used as a model.

– Some houses will be small versions of their own (or of different) villages.

– [In an office] it will be possible to enter the men's room before entering it.

– Residents will begin by relying as much on their houses as on themselves and will eventually come to rely more on their houses than on themselves.

– The episodic will become as hallucinatory and non-hallucinatory.

– The house will relieve one of having to have personality.

– A house may become a substitute for a life.

Arakawa and Madeline Gins

DANIEL LIBESKIND

Berlin, Germany

Opposite
**Extension to the Berlin Museum,
with the Jewish Museum**
Berlin, Germany.
View of the model.

Daniel Libeskind was born in Poland, and qualified as an architect at the Cooper Union School in New York, before going on to study the history and theory of architecture at the University of Essex in England. During the eighties, he emerged as a unique figure in his field, searching for a language that could renew the meaning of architecture by drawing on sources as disparate as music, mathematics and history. His drawings and models, with their complex angular geometry, have contributed to the revival of architecture as drama.

No subject could have lent itself better to an exploration of the darker side of human experience, than the construction of a Jewish Museum as part of the Berlin Museum complex. The building, which is currently being completed, will be an eloquent, dignified and rigorous response to this historic tragedy.

Letter from Berlin
Essay

Today in Germany one constantly hears a particularly depressing comment about architecture and planning: "It's over." What's over? Some would have you believe that the time when vision and dream mattered is over, that the time in which the fatality of the past was transformed into something new by the courage to build has ended. Building is perhaps the only art that is essentially optimistic. For no one can construct the city and its buildings without feeling that they will usher in a better future. Yet today pessimism and a loss of nerve thwart the desire to embrace the future as a challenge. The ghosts of the past are now invoked in an authoritarian mood determined to undermine the extraordinary achievements of post-war Germany.

Since the end of World War II Germany has played a leading role in architecture and urban planning, striving to create fresh environmental alternatives and technically innovative ways of living through building. This tradition of expanding possibilities through realizing dreams has been associated with Germany ever since the great experiments in architecture and planning, beginning with the Werkbund, the Bauhaus, and the Siedlung developments and continuing through the post-war building exhibitions. Invoking poetic rationality Josef Paul Kleihues demonstrated in the recent IBA projects in Berlin that planning can incorporate diverse elements from around the world into the rich mosaic of the city.

Is this legacy about to end? Certain forces now seek to deny the preeminent role that innovative architecture and urban planning have played in

Germany. I believe that the continuity of its tradition of hope is today threatened by reactionary tendencies that seek to eliminate the awareness that Germany has produced truly great visions, buildings, and cities, and that its energy has given real substance to the very premise of European culture.

Some months ago I sat in a hall in Magdeburg at a conference devoted to the planning and building of the newly opened areas in the former DDR. I listened as planners and architects from the East were given the new ABCs that would make them successful in the reunited Germany. The proposed set of rules called for a rigid and reactionary order that employs a seductive simplicity in attacking complex problems; in short, there was to be iron discipline during a time of transition.

The delegates were instructed on the various points of the new order: no new ideas were needed in architecture or urban planning, no dreams, no thoughts, no vision – only silence and conformity. As I sat there amidst the architects and planners of the former DDR, listening with an increasing sense of dismay, I felt a sense of outrage that what was being advocated was a reactionary call to order: be silent, don't dream, relinquish vision, forget individual creativity, follow the rules of the game if you want to build.

This dogmatic and antidemocratic view of society has begun to affect and transform the architectural climate of Germany. Even more distressing is the fact that it is representative of what is now happening in Berlin – not only theoretically but practically in building. Architecture in Berlin is now subjected to a staggering degree of regimentation and control, which is disguised by a rhetoric of order. Arbitrary constraints under the guise of rationalism now exist, which even able architects such as Philip Johnson, Arata Isozaki, and Richard Meier cannot overcome. Six months ago Philip Johnson delivered a public apologia in Berlin for his scheme for the Business Centre at Checkpoint Charlie, explaining that no other modern city would have been able to force him to do such a boring and mediocre design. Without commenting on the aesthetics of these architects, the point is clear: if leading and successful architects find it impossible to produce architecture that would match the great architectural legacy of Berlin, then what hope is there for the younger generation?

It is enough to look at the winning projects in the last three years of competitions in Berlin to see how these new rules are transforming the fascinating diversity of Berlin into banal uniformity. With few exceptions, those buildings now under construction round the city represent an unimaginative regurgitation of bureaucratic administrative formulas subsumed under the banner of rationalism. The style is simple, quick, and sterile, tolerating no deviation in form or material. It provides the perfect background for the emergence of the one-dimensional individual, the individual without qualities.

Berlin is a fascinating montage of conflicting histories, scales, forms, and spaces – a rich mix of substance and imagination. The current criteria of the Senatsbau administration of Berlin are not just basic guidelines to guarantee responsible future development but are authoritarian and repressive edicts. The planning framework no longer covers simple measures or parameters for construction, but actually interferes with the materials, forms, expression, and, finally, the message of architecture. In using stone facades, gable roofs, punched-in windows, invariable grids, unrelenting symmetries, and closed blocks, the buildings and streets conform to one bureaucrat's idea of the good. Recently the winner of the Alexanderplatz competition stated that the city can no longer be built with glass, concrete, and steel, but must be rebuilt in the eternal material of granite.

Life in a pluralistic society involves tremendous vitality and the necessary diversity of experience and views of reality. One of the aspects that made me feel welcome in democratic Germany was the condition of openness that confirmed a fundamental respect for the individual, for initiative, for the different, for the other. Yet today this precious state no longer exists. An intolerance, a fundamentalism, a truly destructive hostility toward the new has crept into the present discourse of architecture and urban planning. A strong polarization based on power and control attempts to further the illusion of unanimity through exclusion.

The belief that architecture has fallen into the wrong hands - capitalist investors, the media, artist-architects, and ignorant people - is itself part of the crisis being decried What is being demanded is a definitive transformation of the city from an all-too-human institution to a perfectly controlled and singular image. Such a nihilistic analysis of history reduces the complexity and mystery of the city to a diagrammatic and lifeless entity.

Glass Pavilion
Exhibition of the Deutscher Werkbund, Cologne, 1914.
Bruno Taut

Planning decisions should be concerned with creating a vital city that looks toward the future. The city is a great spiritual creation of humanity, a collective work that develops the expression of culture, society, and the individual in time and space. Its structure is intrinsically complex; it develops more like a dream than a piece of equipment. The impact of the spiritual, the individual, and the creative cannot be relegated to some outdated past. As long as there are human beings, there will be the possibility of dreaming the impossible and achieving the possible, which is the very essence of humanity.

The dimension of the city is a fundamental structure. As Peter Behrens said: "Architecture, too, strives towards infinity; but more than any other art it is the art that, because of its techniques and purpose, remains bound to tangible materials ... it remains tied to Earth but seeks a spiritual link to the universe." If the creative space of architecture is reduced to some abstract formula of "reducing simple plans and strong elevations" then there is no more possibility for architecture, only for critics who read buildings and build readings. Is the urban realm to be reduced to a nullity by these heartless materialists and spiritless technocrats?

Simple-minded analyses of society, the economy, politics, and architecture cannot deal with the problems of density, ecology, and reconstruction of cities. It is no answer to rummage through the debris of history in order to cartoon some moment within it for further exploitation. In selecting for Berlin and the newly opened lands particular points in history from the nineteenth century, or from the Art Deco period, or even the Third Reich itself, there is a pretence that one can choose one's history as simply as a breakfast cereal.

Any architect or historian might have a preferred period of history. But that is very different from abusing history in order to suppress and politically legislate against other histories and against the present. An architect working in an open society has the responsibility to struggle with the conflicting interpretations of history expressed within the city. To produce meaningful architecture is not to parody history but to articulate it; it is not to erase history but to deal with it. One must take, for example, the existing context in the former DDR seriously, not because one likes the ill-conceived buildings, but because its history and its people must be respected.

The richness and historical heritage of German architecture cannot be purged of everything that is thought to pollute it. The explicit belittlement and dismissal of the art of architecture is a radical denial of the tradition that extends from before Karl Friedrich Schinkel and Peter Behrens and goes beyond Mies Van der Rohe. It includes significant architects such as Hans Scharoun, Bruno Taut, Erich Mendelsohn, and Hans Poelzig. The policy of anti-modernity is a policy against culture itself.

An unethical architecture, whether politically or economically motivated, is unacceptable and deplorable because it is profoundly anti-humanistic – an embodiment of the ideal of mass conformity. The old trick of lumping humanity into a single mass of submissive users in the name of the one and only truth is malignant and dangerous. Those who decry the lack of order only testify to their own confusion and lack of talent. The phrase "the myth of innovation" implies a comparison with those who saw the whole humanistic basis of the 20th century as a myth to be debunked. Something is wrong when architecture is conceived as no more than a technique for adjusting the *Kleinbürger* so completely to the times that he or she no longer feels a desire for anything but silence. The claim that the cities of Sienna and St. Petersburg are products of monotony and repetitiveness is ridiculous since these cities share a unity based on a shared spiritual belief rather than on technocratic legislation.

The desire for a universal national style coupled with the privileging of handicraft is not a refinement of architecture in our time but a dead end. No one involved in architecture can possibly be deluded into believing that contemporary industry and technology will suddenly give way to stone masons hewing obediently according to clear patterns. The present ecological crisis necessitates a serious rethinking of building in relation to materials and functions. The facile cosmetics of corporate architecture are not needed, nor is the banal formalism of 22-metre-high blocks (24 yds) with courtyards and internal green space. Instead we must be concerned with the architectural and human quality of buildings. Mies Van der Rohe's famous adage "God is in the details" has been deliberately misinterpreted. Now technique and details have themselves become gods.

Although we must question and criticize the obvious crass commercialism and pretentious excesses of the 1970s and 1980s, the solution to the complex problems that exist, in Germany and elsewhere, is not to be found by looking fifty years into the past, nor by advocating repetitive anonymity in the future. The answer is not to suppress individual creativity, nor abandon tolerance and diversity. One must never forget or forfeit the universal sanctity of thought and its expression. The architect must be more than a mouthpiece for the prevailing opinion. His soul must have a part in the creative struggle. The intelligence, desire, and ambition of people everywhere should not be underestimated in the task of creatively mastering the challenge of today.

National Gallery
Berlin 1962-1967.
Mies Van der Rohe.

Landsberger Allee
Berlin, Germany.
View of the competition model.

Landsberger Allee and Ringstrasse, Berlin, Germany

The Landsberger Allee project won first prize in 1994 in an international urban design competition. The scheme represents a radical departure from the conventional imposition of rigid block structures. The plan is based on an overall ecological organization which takes into consideration the existing social fabric. It is an approach that is neither traditionally contextual nor a simple replay of the dream of a *tabula rasa*. It proposes an open urban strategy which would immediately produce dramatic architectural interventions, transformations and improvements, both in residential and in working areas.

The entire zone has been conceived as a gateway to the twenty-first century and the forces of change. The Landsberger Allee itself, one of the grandest monumental boulevards of the former GDR, is transformed into a street whose rhythm is related, both visually and architecturally, to the surrounding region.

The future of such areas can no longer be determined by narrow individual interests based on ideology and dogma. They must be seen in the context of the full spectrum of social, political and cultural complexities by which the future is related to the past through the present.

The Berlin Museum with the Jewish Museum

The Jewish Museum won first prize for Daniel Libeskind in an international competition in 1989, and is due to open in 1996. The project seeks to show how the history of Berlin is inseparable from that of its Jewish citizens – two histories which have been tragically intertwined. There were three fundamental aspects to be addressed: the impossibility of representing the history of Berlin without including the history of its Jewish population; the

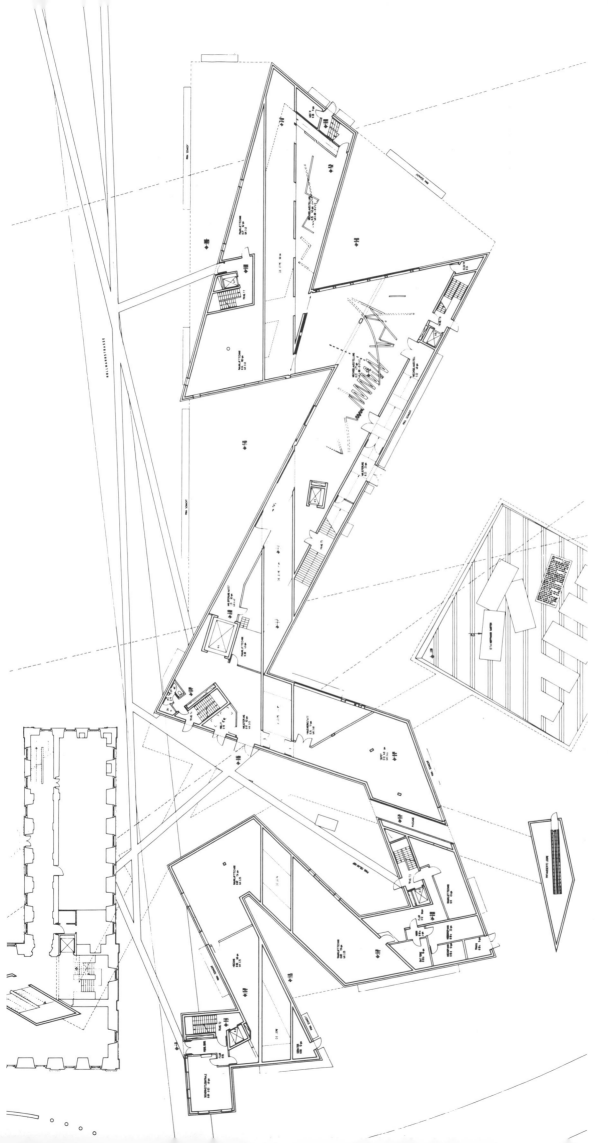

Extension to the Berlin Museum, with the Jewish Museum
Germany.
Ground floor plan.

Opposite
Above
The Jewish Museum under construction.
Below
View of the model.

need to find an architectural project that would physically incorporate the fact of the absence of Jewish life in the city after the Holocaust; and, on an urbanistic level, the need to shed light on the relationship between place and memory in the once divided city.

The new Museum is entered through the old Baroque building. Visitors go down into a basement, where they discover an intersection where three "roads" meet. The first short road leads to a cul-de-sac which forms an acute angle with the Holocaust tower: in this structure will be deposited the last signatures of all those Jews who were deported from the city and murdered. The second road leads to the E.T.A. Hoffman garden, which is composed of pillars symbolizing Jewish exile and emigration. Along the last road, which is also the longest, will be displayed those religious artefacts of the Jewish community that have survived. This road leads the visitor back to the main galleries by a staircase.

At the heart of the building, then, is an empty space: an impenetrable structure, criss-crossed by empty bridges leading from one galery to another. Visitors are led around this space of absence, which testifies to the eradication of Berlin's Jewish community.

BERNARD TSCHUMI

New York, USA
Paris, France

During the seventies, Bernard Tschumi was one of the first to introduce material from other disciplines into architecture: texts (the James Joyce garden), cinema (a plan based on the ballet scene from *Frankenstein*), and journalism (defenestration as an architectural experience) in his series of witty and provocative manifesto pieces, the *Manhattan Transcripts*.

With projects such as the Parc de la Villette in Paris or the Groningen video gallery, he has continued to assert the precedence of event over architectural context, defining architecture as "a pleasurable and sometimes violent confrontation between space and activity".

The Architecture of the Event
Essay

Architecture has always been as much about the event that takes place in a space as about the space itself. In today's world where railway-stations become museums and churches become nightclubs, we must come to terms with the complete interchangeability of form and function, the loss of traditional or canonical cause-and-effect relationships as sanctified by modernism. Function does not follow form, form does not follow function, or fiction for that matter. However, form and function certainly interact, if only to produce a shock effect.

If "shock" can no longer be produced by the succession and juxtaposition of façades and lobbies, maybe it can be produced by the juxtaposition of events that take place behind these façades in these spaces.

If "the respective contamination of all categories, the constant substitutions, the confusion of genres," as described by critics of the right and the left alike (from Andreas Huyssens to Jean Baudrillard), is the new direction of our times, it may well be used to one's advantage, to the advantage of a general rejuvenation of architecture. If architecture is both concept and experience, space and use, structure and superficial image (nonhierarchically), then architecture should cease to separate these categories and should merge them into unprecedented combinations of programmes and spaces. "Cross-programming," "transprogramming," "disprogramming": these concepts stand for the displacement and mutual contamination of terms.

My own work in the seventies constantly reiterated the thesis that there was no architecture without event, without action, without activities, without functions; architecture was to be seen as the combination of spaces, events and movements, without any hierarchy or precedence among these concepts. Needless to say, the hierarchical cause-and-effect relation between function

Opposite
Parc de La Villette
Paris, France.

and form is one of the great certainties of architectural thinking – it lies behind that reassuring *idée reçue* of community life that tells us that we live in houses "designed to answer to our needs" or in cities planned as machines to live in. And the cosy connotations of this *geborgenheit* notion go against both the real "pleasure" of architecture, in its unexpected combinations of terms, and the reality of contemporary urban life, in its most stimulating, as well as unsettling, facets. Hence, in works like the *Manhattan Transcripts*, the definition of architecture could not be form, or walls, but had to be the combination of heterogeneous and incompatible terms.

The incorporation of the terms "event" and "movement" was no doubt influenced by situationist discourse and the '68 era. "Les événements," as they were called, were events, not only in action, but also in thought. Erecting a barricade (function) in a Paris street (form) is not quite equivalent to being a flaneur (function) in that same street (form). Dining (function) in a university hall (form) is not quite equivalent to reading or swimming in it. Here, all hierarchical relationships between form and function cease to exist.

This unlikely combination of events and spaces was charged with subversive capabilities, for it challenged both the function and the space: such confrontation parallels the Surrealists' meeting of the sewing machine and the umbrella on the dissecting-table. We find it today in Tokyo, with its multiple programmes scattered throughout the floors of the high-rise buildings: department-store, museum, health-club, railway-station, putting-greens on the roof. And we will find it in the programmes of the future, where airports are also simultaneously amusement-arcades, athletic-facilities, cinemas, and so on. Regardless of whether they are the result of chance combinations or of the pressures of ever rising land prices, such non-causal relationships between form and function, or space and action, go beyond poetic confrontations of unlikely bedfellows.

Foucault, as was recalled in an excellent recent book by John Rajchman, expanded the use of the term "event" in a manner that went beyond the single action or activity. He spoke of "events of thought." I would suggest that the future of architecture today lies in the construction of such events. For Foucault, an event is not simply a logical sequence of words or actions, but rather "the moment of erosion, collapse, questioning or problematization of the very assumptions of the setting within which a drama may take place - occasioning the chance or possibility of another, different setting" (Rajchman). The event is seen here as a turning-point, not an origin or an end (as opposed to propositions such as "form follows function").

After Foucault, Derrida expanded on the definition of "event," calling it "the emergence of a disparate multiplicity" in a text about the folies of the Parc de la Villette. I had constantly insisted, in our discussions and elsewhere, that these points called folies were points of activities, of programmes, of events. Derrida elaborated this concept, proposing the possibility of an "architecture of the event" that would "eventualize," or open up, what in our history or tradition is understood to be fixed, essential, monumental.

Derrida had also suggested earlier that the word "event" shared roots with "invention." I would like to associate it with the notion of "shock," a shock that in order to be effective in our mediated culture, in our culture of images, must go beyond the definition of Walter Benjamin and combine the idea of function or action with that of image. Indeed, architecture finds itself in a unique situation: it is the only discipline that by definition combines concept and experience, image and use, image and structure. Philosophers can write, mathematicians can develop virtual spaces, but architects are the only ones who are the prisoners of that hybrid art where the image hardly ever exists without combined activity.

It is my contention that far from being a field suffering from its inability to question its own structures and foundations, architecture is the field where the greatest discoveries will take place in the next century. The very heterogeneity of the definition of architecture – space, action and movement – makes it that event, that place of shock, or that place of the invention of ourselves. The event is the place where the rethinking and reformulation of the different elements of architecture (many of which have resulted in, or added to, contemporary social inequities) may lead to their solution. By definition, it is the place of the combination of difference.

Of course, it is not by imitating the past that this will happen. It is also not going to happen by simple commenting through design on the various dislocations and uncertainties of our contemporary condition. I do not believe it is possible, nor that it makes sense, to design buildings that formally attempt to blur traditional structures, i.e. that display forms that lie somewhere between abstraction and figuration, or somewhere between structure and ornament, or that are cut up, dislocated for aesthetic reasons. Architecture is not an illustrative art; it does not illustrate theories.

You cannot design a new definition of the city and its architecture. But you may be able to design the conditions that will make it possible for this nonhierarchical, nontraditional society to happen. By understanding the nature of our contemporary circumstances and the media processes that go with them, architects are in a position to construct conditions that will create a new city and new relationships between spaces and events.

Architecture is not about the conditions of design, but about the design of conditions. Or, to paraphrase Paul Virilio, our object today is not to fulfil the conditions of construction, but to achieve the construction of conditions that will dislocate the most traditional and regressive aspects of our society and simultaneously reorganize these elements in the most liberating way, where our experience becomes the experience of events organized and strategized through architecture. Strategy is a key word today in architecture. No more masterplans, no more locating in a fixed place, but a new heterotopia. That is what our cities are striving towards, and here we architects must help them by intensifying the rich collision of events and spaces.

Tokyo and New York only appear chaotic; in reality, they mark the appearance of a new urban structure, a new urbanity. Their confrontations and combinations of elements may provide us with the event, the shock, that I very much hope will make the architecture of our cities a turning-point in culture and in society.

Folies in the Parc de La Villette
Paris, France.

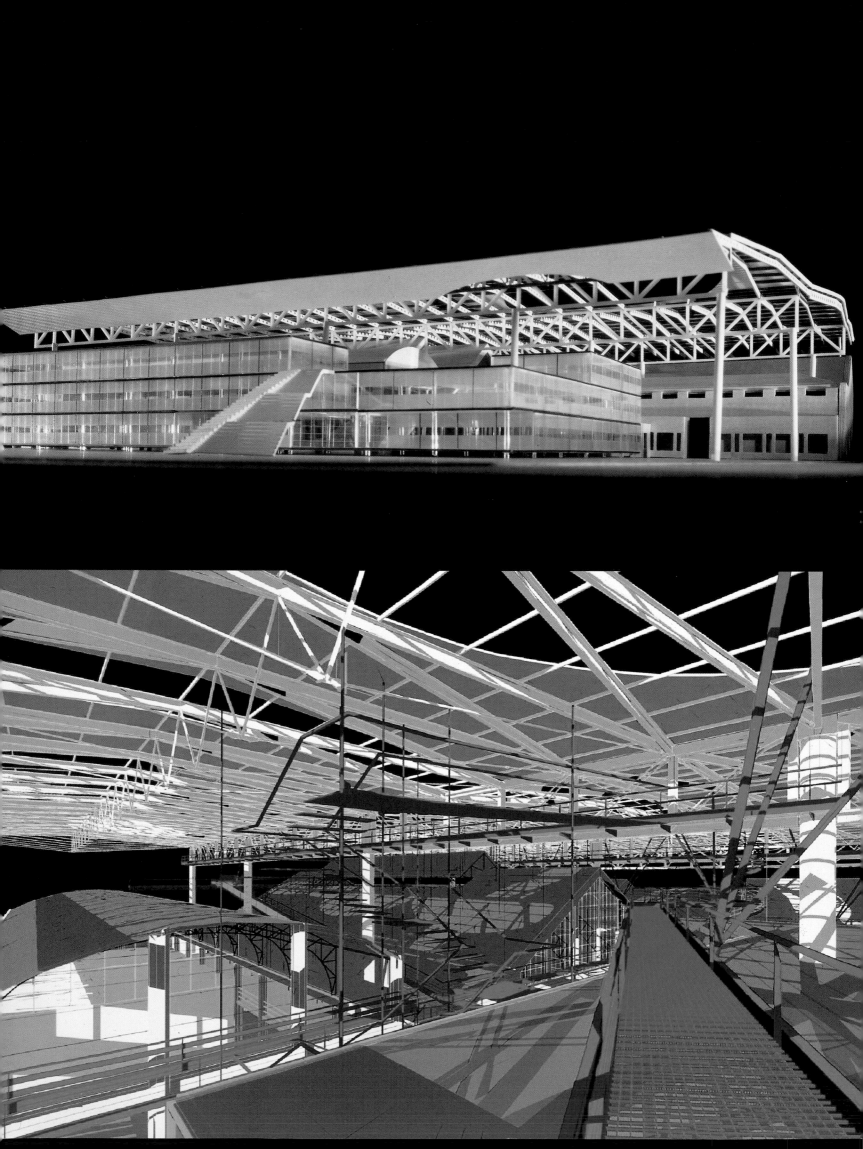

National Studio for Contemporary Arts, Tourcoing, France

The complex is intended to be precise and rational in its conception, yet richly poetic in its spatial diversity. The great steel roof, traversed by "clouds" of light, floats above the old tiled roofs, creating a new plane of reference, an artificial sky ("artifi-ciel"). Not only does this huge roof generate the new poetic space of the "in-between", but it provides a pragmatic solution to problems of climate, energy and information. The scale and presence of this horizontal space relativizes the concepts of inside and outside in relation to the old building. The "in-between" iself becomes a concept, condensing different fields of investigation: teaching, performance, and research; art and cinema; music and image. This multi-functional space, which is intended to "cover" the event (whether it be a congress, a concert, an athletics meeting, or an exhibition, not to mention their thousands of visitors), is one possible model for the new "urban" spaces of the 21st century.

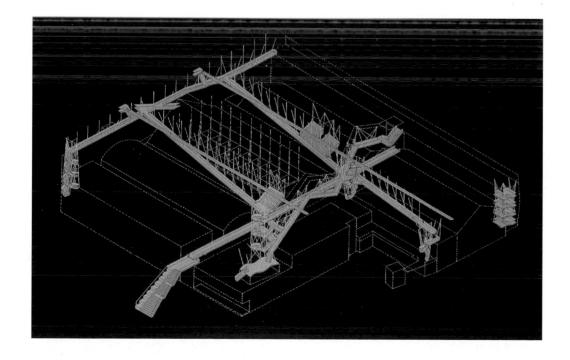

National Studio for Contemporary Arts
Tourcoing, France
Axonometric showing the circulation paths.

Opposite

Above
View of the model.
Below
Interior perspective.

39

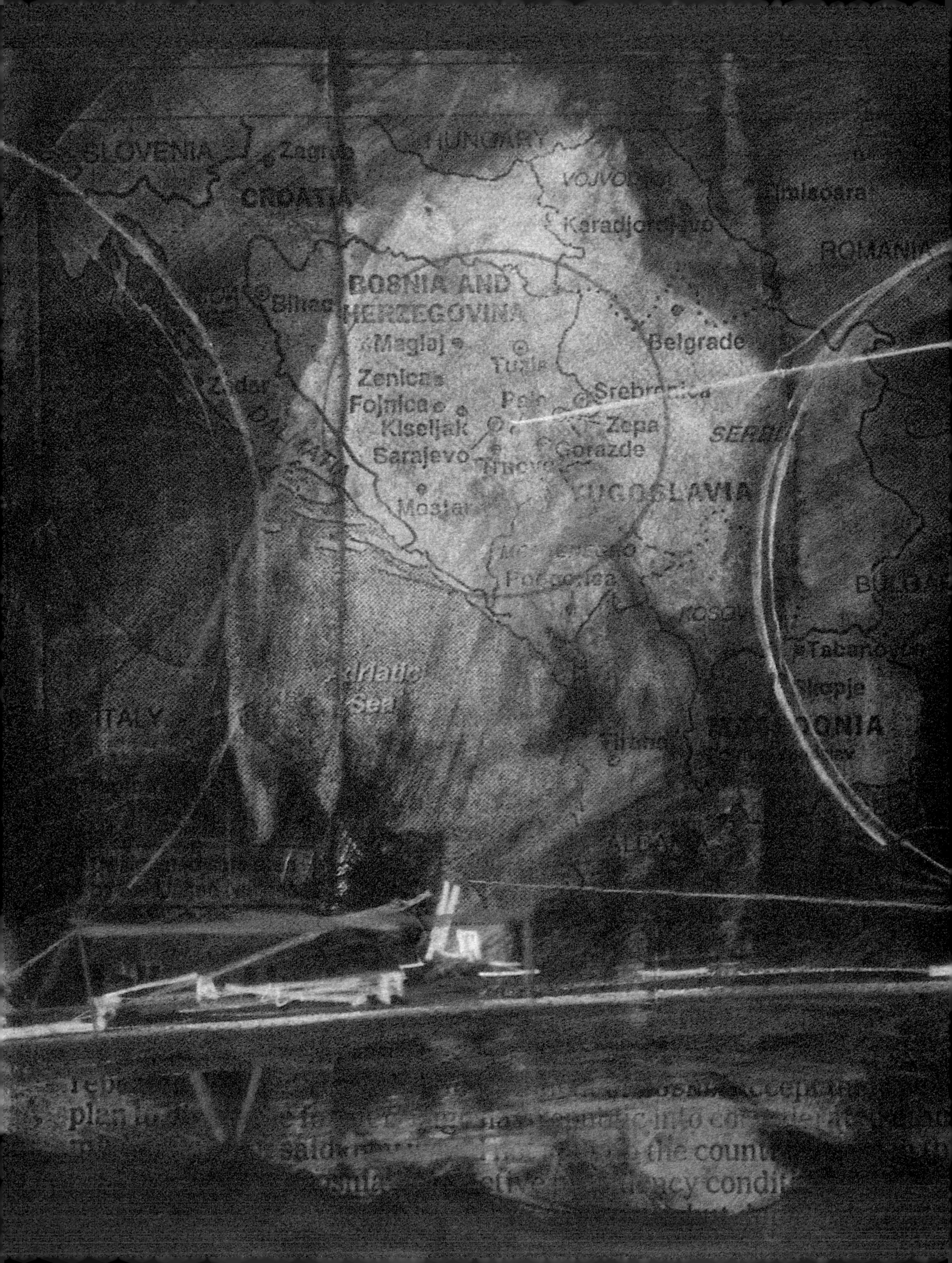

SLOVENIA

Zagreb

HUNGARY

VOJVODINA

Karadjordjevo

CROATIA

ROMANIA

Bihac

BOSNIA AND
HERZEGOVINA

Maglaj

Belgrade

Zenica

Tuzla

Zadar

Fojnica

Pale

Srebrenica

Kiseljak

Zepa

SERBIA

Sarajevo

Gorazde

Nuevo

YUGOSLAVIA

Mostar

Montenegro

Podgorica

BULGARIA

KOSOVO

Adriatic
Sea

Tabanovce

Skopje

ITALY

MACEDONIA

Tirana

ALB.

plen

the coun

ncy condi

LEBBEUS WOODS

New York, USA

Lebbeus Woods stood out as an original figure against the backdrop of futile post-modernism that enshrouded New York in the 1980s. He reinvented architecture by integrating time and wear into his projects. His vision of building was realistic, not to say pessimistic. His manifesto-projects were bathed in an expressionistic atmosphere as they sought to describe a mechanistic world at the limits of science fiction: an ageing, run-down universe, brought to the verge of ruin. In the 1990s, his work has taken a political turn, provoked by the war between Serbia and Bosnia. Woods' recent projects put architecture on a war footing.

War and architecture, Bosnia Freestate
Essay

Architecture has always attempted to codify, by the definition of an analogous spatial order, the best of what any society possesses, from the material and technological to the intellectual and poetical.

Present society offers a richer, more complex and in many ways more conflicting and paradoxical spectrum of choices than any before it. As a result, demands are made on architecture to provide an analogous, accommodating structuring of space. However, there has been a qualitative change in the historical mission of architecture, owing chiefly to the increasing complexity of social relationships and interactions, but also to the radical collapse of time in which social exchange takes place. It will no longer be sufficient for architecture merely to accommodate or express ideas and events, for this requires a historical distance or objectivity that no longer exists. Rather, architecture can only participate in social transformations, becoming more dynamic, fluid and even more kinetic than it has ever been before.

Social institutions are increasingly polarized into those supporting choice for as many people as possible, and those working against it. The projects presented here attempt to define new types of spatial order, corresponding to the paradoxical and conflicting events and ideas that continue to shape human society.

The Wall, Bosnia Freestate is conceived for a besieged state with a history of being on the periphery of contending empires and absorbing them into a model multi-cultural society. At the same time, it proposes a type of heterarchical urban and architectural order that results from the accumulation of small-scale elements not designed to be together, using new principles of spatial construction and organization. It functions on the principle of absorbing and transforming the enemy's land-based attacks by the complexity of

Opposite
The Wall, Bosnia Free State
Drawing.

41

its construction. Its complex, discontinuous series of spaces once entered cannot be easily exited, and the lack of a spatial hierarchy prevents any form of mass military action. Small-scale encounters lead inevitably to less hostile forms of exchange and the combatants and their camp followers gradually build up a complex urban network – a city – in the space between contending nation-states.

Zagreb Free-Zone comprises a series of structures that appear in the streets of a newly-forming state seeking a transition from centralized state

The Wall, Bosnia Freestate
Drawing.

The Wall, Bosnia Freestate is a massive structure that defends the territory of a people who have suffered a medieval form of aggression with modern weapons.

socialism to an as-yet-undefined form of open society. The structures have no pre-determined meaning or function, and yet contain spaces with a potential for inhabitation. Their non-Cartesian form, however, frustrates conventional ways of inhabitation, and, at the same time invites and facilitates the invention of new ones. They comprise a city-within-a-city, a free-zone, that corresponds to communities emerging in the world today which are based on the increase of personal choice and responsibility through non-traditional uncontrolled forms of exchange.

FRANÇOIS ROCHE

Paris, France

Opposite
House in the trees,
La Croix-Saint-Ouen, France.

A period as a member of the punk movement and a sojourn as a hermit in the desert are among the stages that make up the unusual career of François Roche. Roche graduated as an architect in 1987. He first began to be noticed in France in the early 1990s, thanks to his combative public pronouncements. Turbulent and polemical, he was an unsettling presence in the staid, insecure world of French architecture, whose dreams had been brought down to earth in no uncertain manner, now that the "Grands Travaux" state building programme was completed. Roche is both pragmatic and irreverent. He has no time for rules and conventions which seem to him out of place or out of date. He reaffirms the social function of architecture, and seeks to refocus attention on domains which are distinctly less glorious than the monumental constructions of the preceding decade. For Roche, the role of architecture is to confront the challenge of housing and public space, in a society that is prey to considerable social problems.

The shadow of the chameleon
Essay

I know people who are born into truth. I am not like them. Some have a creed, a mission, a philosophy, others plagiarize counterfeit ideologies. I do not belong to either camp. What I am interested in are the multiple, complex choices that are opened up, once architecture has put off its princely autonomy, and at last agrees to learn from those areas of experience to which it had tried to dictate. But do not think I want to take pride in seeing while all around me are blind. Sight is worth nothing, if it is not shared.

Architects have invariably represented the domination of man over nature, of the city over the ecosystem, of the built over the un-built. In the end, land has served as at best, a found object, at worst, an alibi, there to be exploited. Our profession has become isolated, egotistical and self-absorbed, restricting its activity to stylistic exercises and in-fighting. The architecture which was born out of utopian dreams never managed to cast off its perverse sclerosis, its halo of progressivist prediction and a better future...

In a system whose only preoccupation is with its own image, few suspect that the architectural object has imploded to such an extent that it is useless to try and cling to what it was or what it should be. Situated at the intersection of political interests, economic, territorial and social tensions, spurred on by continuous technological and industrial change, it is eternally condemned to be torn apart by competing demands. And yet there is no justification for drawing the eclectic conclusion from this state of affairs, and siding blindly with

omnipresent chaos. On the contrary, the greater the confusion, the more urgent are the ethical and political choices which would be capable of reviving the processes of meaning and stemming the wastage that surrounds us today.

The interpretation of Place and Context should be the very essence of the architectural act.

Creeds and individualisms should be contorted, infiltrated and inserted in and against that which they were seeking to destroy.

Stylistic effects, intelligently reworked, should be sensitive to existing territorial conditions: to climate, wind, wear and tear, the seasons, the built and the un-built, time and raw materials, reduced to their bare essentials.

At last we should learn how to do LESS so that we can work WITH.

We must reinvent an architecture that would be animistic, sensual, primitive, political, an antidote to blind and hyper-active modernity, both lucid and optimistic in the face of anxiety as our planet burns; we must reinvent architecture, not in order to launch a new style, a new school, a new theoretical hegemony, but so as to redefine the basis of our profession, in today's conditions.

Whether landscape is urban, suburban, natural or cultivated, it has its own topographical, emotional and climatic codes. It is through these places and these contexts that we must work. Clearly, their constitution can only be discovered by spending time in them, sometimes only by living with them... The "genetic code of territoriality" is not a recipe that can be printed out, a politically-correct label for yuppies in search of an ideology, but a process of entering into contact, which must be enacted afresh for each intervention.

Do not get me wrong: there is nothing pastoral or fashionably green about the approach I advocate. It is not a return to nature for the Sunday supplements, vegetarianism as architectural alibi. The process of infiltration must employ means that match the scale of the territories to be confronted. The re-education of our own vital instincts that will follow must be equally radical.

This plea for an architecture of time and wear, of sensuality and of meaning, that is both territorial and human, would have no substance, if it could not draw on new skills and techniques in cartography, geology, the reasoned assessment of preconditions and the evolution of technologies. The aim is not to produce a contemporary version of the sterile, reheated recipes of the Academy, but fresh fruit and fresh vegetables, fresh meat and fish. An architecture at the cutting edge of art – and history – at the end of this century.

Its skin must be light-sensitive to its immediate context. Its basic functions must be rethought. In this way, architecture can limit its tendency to glorious isolation, and learn to respond to variations in climate, atmosphere, topography and custom. It must sum up nothing that it has not already transformed.

It is imperative that we stay close to what can revive our sense of responsibility, both for the sake of our own survival, and for that of our union with the elements. In the end, isn't the Aristotelian world of appearances and artefacts just as valid as the world of ideas and concepts? All we need to do is come to terms with the real, which is still, despite everything, our only haven, so that our work can intercede for us between our desires and the world they were supposed to dominate.

Opposite
Renovation of building n°48
Sarcelles, France.

Above
Cross section.
Below
Perspective

Left
Elevation.

2. PERFORMANCES

"I may be of lower than average intelligence; but I am well-informed."
R. Buckminster Fuller

Since the dawn of the industrial revolution, technology and science have played an increasingly important role in building. From the Crystal Palace* to the Eiffel Tower, from the skyscraper to the geodesic dome, architecture has attempted to overcome the constraints of solidity and gravity by using ever more delicate structures, larger spans, higher performance materials. The ensuing pact with the engineers and the search for maximum efficiency gave rise to a puritanical attitude to form that, seen as the direct result of necessary constraints, was cold and neutral: beauty as efficiency.

But it soon became obvious that rigorous procedures could produce other, very different kinds of work and that technology had the potential to create new, original forms.

There is no doubt that the Lem that NASA sent to the moon in 1969 came as a shock to the purists: how could the most advanced technology have produced such a shaggy object?

The projects presented here prove, if such proof were needed, that high-tech and the continuing search for technical innovation and performance are compatible with a genuinely free imagination. ■

Opposite
Torre de Collserola
Barcelona, Spain.
Sir Norman Foster

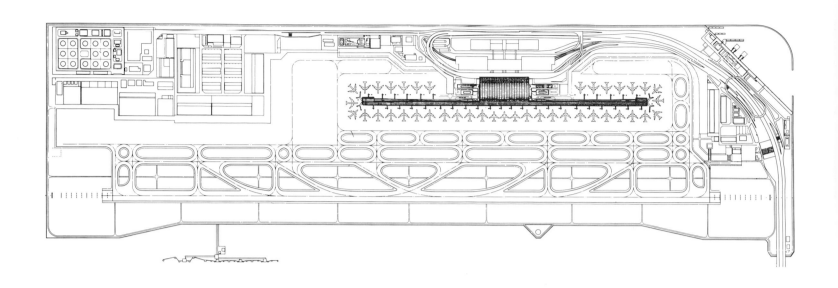

RENZO PIANO

Genoa, Italy
Paris, France

Renzo Piano belongs to a tradition of architects who are above all builders, for whom the primacy of materials and their deployment leads to the patient and detailed search for the solution that is best adapted to each particular problem. Whence the constant, craftsman-like inventiveness of his architecture. From the Pompidou Centre in Paris (1971-77) which made him famous, to his experiments with local workshops for renovating old buildings, from his prototype car for Fiat to the steamships he designed for a Californian collector, Renzo Piano has always been faithful to his own lights. In his work, the quiet perfectionism of his "trade" counts for so much more than the spectacular gesture.

Kansai International Airport

In order to protect the coastal enviroment and to avoid both pollution and the protests of ecologists, Kansai Airport was constructed on an artificial island 4.37 km x 1.25 km (4,779 yds x 1,367 yds), situated 5 km (a little more than 3 miles) out into Osaka Bay.

It was Renzo Piano's passion for this unique project which helped him to win the competition. The transition from the magical state of air travel to the realities of arrival on the island suggested playing on the relation between nature and technical efficiency. This idea is realised in concrete terms as two natural planted "valleys", one of which separates the runway from the terminal, and the other the terminal from the roadways leading to the town. These two valleys echo the serenity of the bay and its islands.

The form of the terminal itself was derived from the study of airflow dynamics. New methods of computer-assisted analysis which enable the visualization of airflow patterns, implied a more supple structure and provided the basis for the creation of new irregular forms, possessing a complex mobility. The fluid curves of the terminal building are intended to recall the forms of aeroplanes.

There is no facade in the traditional sense of the term. Land and architecture are gently integrated one with the other. The interior space and the embarcation piers are designed for maximum transparency. The passengers are thus in contact with the reality of runway and machine. The special character of the building derives from this balance between nature and technology.

Opposite
Kansai International Airport, Japan.

Above
Master plan.
Below
Aerial view of the island.

Kansai International Airport Japan.
Computer analysis of air flows on which the form of the roof is based.

51

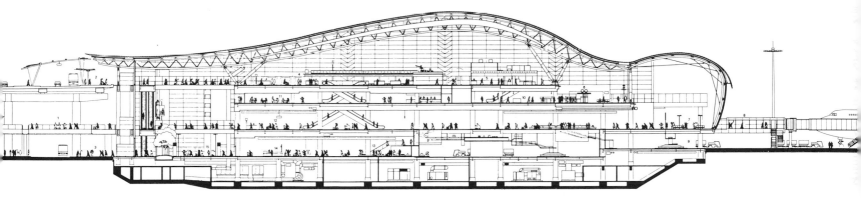

Kansaï International Airport,
Japan.

Above
Cross section of the main terminal building.
Below left
Elevation, runway side.
Below right
Interior.

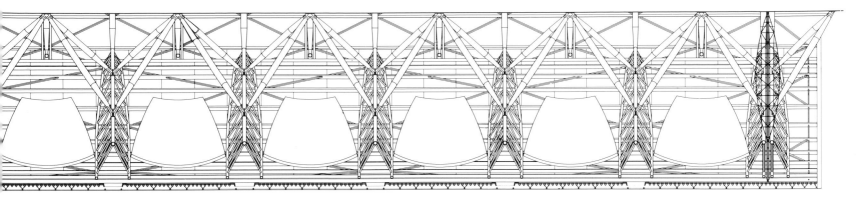

Above
Longitudinal axonometric of the structure.
Below
Check-in area.

Overleaf
The terminal at night.

NICHOLAS GRIMSHAW

London, Great Britain

After studying architecture at Edinburgh University, Nicholas Grimshaw was an outstanding student at the Architectural Association in London, where he obtained his diploma in 1965. His early partnership with Terry Farrell was dissolved when the latter decided to embrace post-modernism. Grimshaw, on the other hand, has always been driven by his determination to explore the resources offered by industrial modes of production, and to design buildings which feel incontrovertibly "right". Whence the sense of restraint that pervades all his most characteristic projects. He has often been called on to design working spaces (the Vitra factory in Weil am Rhein, the Financial Times printing works). The attention he pays to the "human" aspect of such buildings moderates any tendency to technical expressivism. Yet his monumental structure for Waterloo Station in London is undeniably spectacular in the huge curve it defines to follow the line of the tracks. As for the Berlin stock exchange, the very scale of the project seems to have led the architect to address new urban and architectural problems.

Berlin Stock Exchange,
Germany.
Aerial view of the model.

Opposite
Computer-generated perspective.

Berlin Stock Exchange, Germany

The project for the Ludwig Erhard Haus, which will house the Berlin stock exchange and communications centre, and which is due to be completed in 1997, was conceived in response to three specific criteria. First, in order to avoid an excessively tall building, it was necessary to use all the available ground area on the irregularly-shaped site. Second, a direct relationship was to be established between the inner life of the building and the life of the city outside. Third, the public spaces were to be arranged along a gently curving inner "street".

The project was also designed to achieve low energy consumption, reasonable running costs and extremely low pollution levels.

The offices on the upper floors are organized around two unheated triangular atria, which serve to temper the continental climate of Berlin and to bring natural light into the very heart of the building. The inner streets and atria combine to produce a spectacular array of changing perspectives.

Waterloo International Terminal, London, Great Britain

The functions of the Waterloo International Terminal are analagous to those of an airport, and it has most of the services and facilities one would associate with such a building. Yet it is still very much a railway station, a heroic edifice erected on a city-centre site and hemmed in by constraints, less than ten minutes from Trafalgar Square : the first monument of a new era in rail transport.

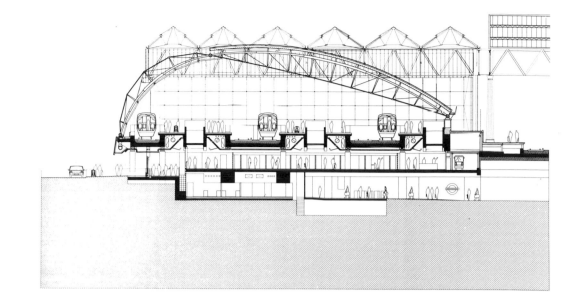

Waterloo International Terminal Station
London, Great Britain.

Above
Cross-section.
Below
Interior.

Opposite
View of the roof.

The roof provides both the greatest technical challenge and the high-point of the drama. It runs for 400 m (437 yds) in a sinuous tapering line determined by the topography of the site and the layout of the tracks. Its strangeness – the asymmetry of its forms – is not wilfully aesthetic, but is determined by the position of a track which runs along the western boundary of the site. The form's inflexion is necessary to create enough height beneath it for a train to pass. Trains approach the terminal from this side. The facade is clad in glass and its form is emphasized by the external structure. It functions as an enormous window onto Westminster and the Thames for arriving passengers.

SIR NORMAN FOSTER

London, Great Britain

Over the last twenty years, Sir Norman Foster has created many architectural landmarks: the museum-hangar of the Sainsbury centre, the Swindon Renault factory, both in Great Britain, and the tower of the Hong Kong and Shanghai Bank in Hong Kong, are among the masterworks of the closing decades of the century. Sir Norman is certainly the purest of the so-called "high-tech" architects, and has made the most persuasive case for faith in technical progress. He has collaborated – and continues to collaborate – with the best engineers: Buckminster Fuller, Jean Prouvé, Tony Fitzpatrick. His buildings feature subtle articulations and finely-drawn structures. They create vast, well-lit spaces, in their search for formal expression: a puritanical aesthetic which owes much to zen, both the zen of archery and that of motorcycle maintenance.

Torre de Collserola, Barcelona, Spain

This telecommunications tower was built to coincide with the Olympic Games. It is a symbol of Barcelona's determination to ally itself with modernity through the creation of a "monumental technological element". The tower rises to 288 metres (315 yds) above ground level, 440 metres (481 yds) above sea level. There is a public gallery and a glass elevator. Its distinctive shape is now a dominant presence, high above the city and its bay.

Reichstag, New Parliament, Berlin, Germany

The Reichstag has had a troubled history from the outset. It was built amid arguments between the architect Wallot and Chancellor Bismarck, burnt down in 1933, and remained abandoned until the sixties when Paul Baumgarten renovated it for sporadic use.

With the reunification of Germany and the decision to transfer the German Parliament from Bonn to Berlin, an open competition for its redevelopment was organized. Sir Norman Foster and Partners were the outright winners, with a design that was both monumental and subtle. A new roof over the original edifice was to define a raised plaza surrounding the building, which would give direct access to the first-floor level. The plenary chamber is circular in form and partially sunk below ground level.

This scheme has since been considerably modified, and the new roof has been abandoned in favour of a plan to rebuild the original cupola – the very cupola which caused Wallot so many problems. Sir Norman has put forward several different propositions for its reconstruction. If the project succeeds, it will be both a monument in its own right, and a symbol of the new Berlin.

Opposite
Torre de Collserola
Barcelona, Spain.

Page 62
Renovation of the Reichstag
Berlin, Germany.

Above
Winning competition entry: a vast roof covers the whole building and extends over the Spree to the North.
Centre
Second project: the roof has been reduced and covers only the plenary chamber.
Below
Third project: the chamber is covered by a glass dome.

Page 63
Renovation of the Reichstag
Berlin, Germany.

Loft
Dome of the original building.
Centre and right
Two variations of the new dome.
Below
The new parliament at night (photomontage).

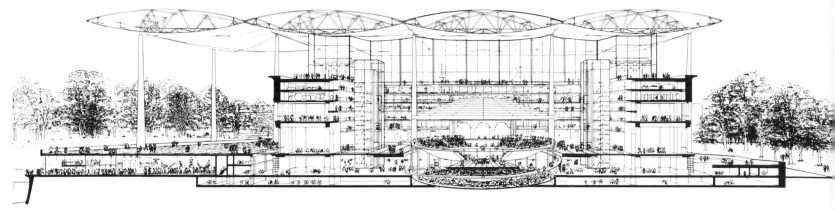

Schnitt Nord-Süd

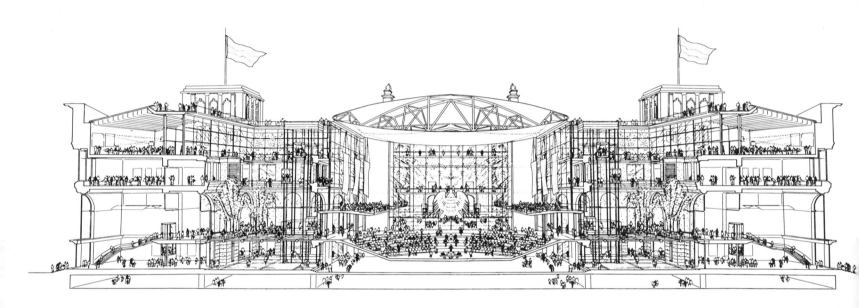

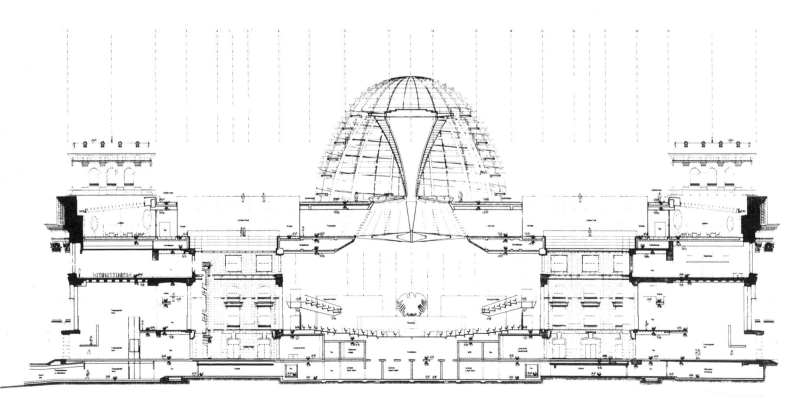

Schnitt CC

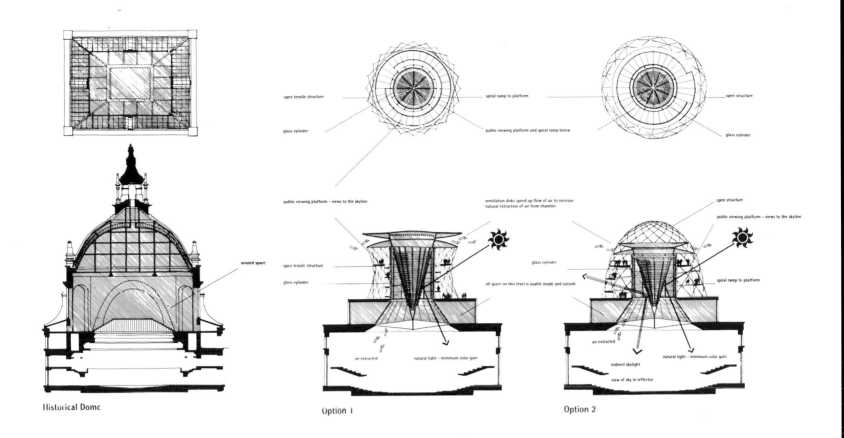

open tensile structure

glass cylinder

spiral ramp to platform

public viewing platform and spiral ramp below

open structure

glass cylinder

public viewing platform - views to the skyline

ventilation disks speed up flow of air to increase natural extraction of air from chamber

open structure

public viewing platform - views to the skyline

unused space

open tensile structure

glass cylinder

all space on this level is usable inside and outside

glass cylinder

spiral ramp to platform

air extracted

natural light - minimum solar gain

air extracted

indirect skylight

natural light - minimum solar gain

view of sky in reflector

Historical Dome

Option 1

Option 2

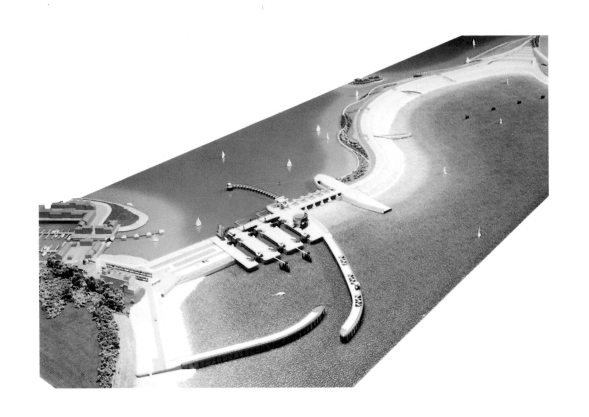

ALSOP & STÖRMER

London, Great Britain

William Alsop trained at a time when British architecture was still in the shadow of Archigram* and the quasi-mythical figure of Cedric Price*. Alsop first achieved recognition in the early 1980s with bizarre high-tech projects that reflected his colourful and outlandish imagination. In his buildings, Alsop tries to marry technical rigour to the expressive freedom of the plastic arts. Thus he "paints" his designs before he draws them. His buildings in Hamburg and Marseille are major urban landmarks, thanks to their powerful, dynamic and highly-coloured presence.

Cardiff Barrage, Cardiff, Great Britain

For the Cardiff barrage, Alsop & Störmer deployed all their skills in both architecture and landscape design, to turn what might have been merely a utilitarian piece of civil engineering into a gigantic work of art. The barrage carries a new road running into the centre of Cardiff, via the dockside of the Victorian suburb of Penarth. The structure curves across the valley; en route, the user discovers a series of architectural "events", whether he is travelling by car or on foot. Brightly coloured structural elements, groves of specially selected plants, picnic areas, fishing piers, and even an artificial island close to the inland side. The aim is to create an architectural drama that will appeal to a wide cross-section of the public, and that will act as a focus for tourists, as well as for the local population.

Le Grand Bleu, Marseille, France

The Grand Bleu is the Regional Government Headquarters for the Department of the Bouches-du-Rhône. The simplicity of its structure – two rectangular sections, administrative blocks and an assembly hall in the shape of a cigar, all joined together by bridges and suspended walkways – creates a series of unexpected spaces and experiences. As they pass through the atria that punctuate the building, employees and members of the public discover the sky above and the activity of the great hall below. The materials employed are simple ones – concrete, glass, wood and steel. But they are used to create a zoomorphic expressionism, which can take even the most jaded visitor by surprise.

Opposite
Above
Cardiff Barrage
Cardiff Bay, Great Britain.
Aerial view of the model.
Below
Visitors' Pavilion.

**Le Grand Bleu, Regional Government
Headquarters of the Bouches-du-Rhône**
Marseille, France.

Opposite
Atrium and walkways.

Right
Cross-section.
Below
General view.

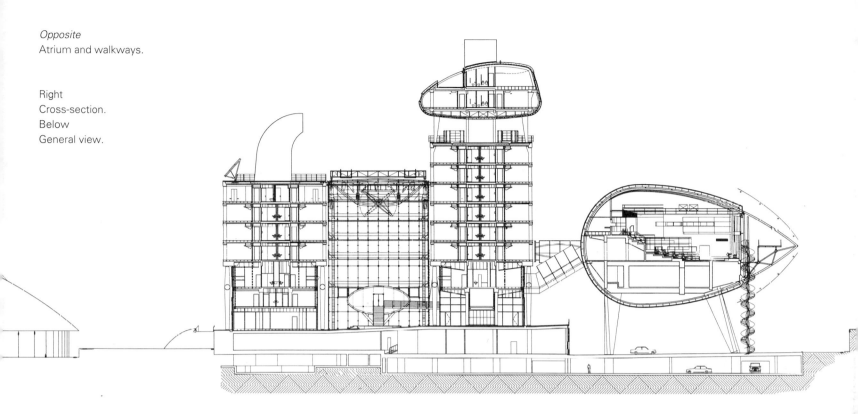

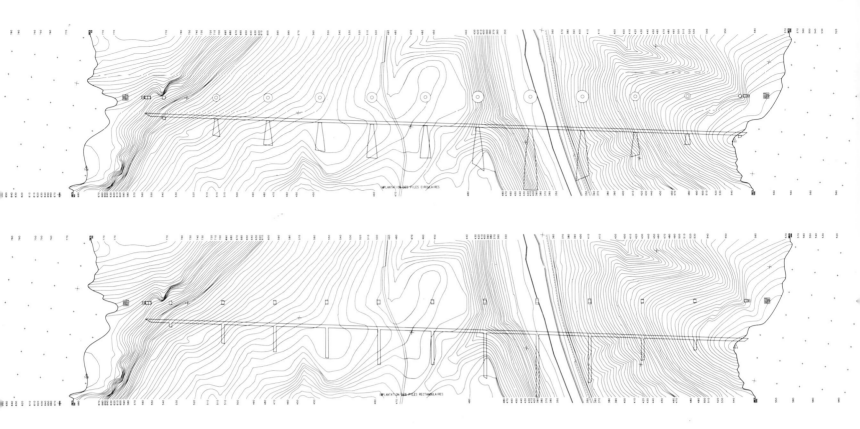

IMPLANTATION DES PILES CIRCULAIRES

IMPLANTATION DES PILES RECTANGULAIRES

JACQUES HONDELATTE

Bordeaux, France

Jacques Hondelatte occupies a special place in the French architectural world. Once he had finished his studies, he chose to settle in Bordeaux, a city that, since the war, has been home to a whole generation of talented modernist architects. There, he acquired a reputation for unusual, innovative projects – a 70 m (77 yds)-long house, an inward-looking student hostel clad in shiny metal – that were the product of an original approach in which imagination and text were more important than accurate plans ("I draw", Hondelatte has said, "once the project is completed").

This freedom of approach excludes neither logic nor technical innovation. It is this vision which enables him to go beyond traditional limits, as in his bold proposal for the Millau viaduct, which seems to have resulted from an improbable collaboration between the two Morandis (the painter and the great engineer).

Viaduct over the Tarn, Aveyron, France

For the point where the A75 motorway is to cross the Tarn Valley, linking the Causse Rouge to the north with the Larzac plateau to the south, a viaduct was chosen, in order to meet constraints of both economy and efficiency. This solution also has the advantage of avoiding an invasive road network.

There can be no question of camouflaging a construction that is 2,600 metres (2,843 yds) long and which rises 270 metres (295 yds) above the floor of the valley. The result must therefore be conceived as a work of art, whose presence will inevitably have an enormous impact on the landscape. Jacques Hondelatte was well aware of this, and studied all the various possibilities, rejecting first of all any that involved piers or pylons which would rise above the level of the surrounding hills (on the model of the Golden Gate Bridge in San Francisco). He also refused to exploit the opportunity to erect some ultimate monument to modernity, and indulge in a brilliant and flashy technological tour de force.

Instead he chose a "single, simple, regular" construction, with uniform spans and beam lengths. The fundamental decision was to have the two traffic lanes one above the other, within a thick, hollow beam, to be made either of concrete or of steel. The dimensions of the roadway and those of the piers have been chosen on the basis of analogy, so as to fuse together rather than articulate separately the different parts of the structure.

The substantial winds that will buffet the viaduct led to the choice of thin rectangular shafts at the head. Further study of circular constructions (silos, radio towers) also inspired a variant form, with circular piers on simple foundations, like soft cones or giant bottles, that blend into the forms of the neighbouring causses.

Opposite
Viaduct over theTarn
Aveyron, France.

Above
Two variations of the load-bearing structure: one based on columns with a circular section, the other on rectangular columns.
Below
Aerial view (photomontage).

Overleaf
Aerial view of the viaduct in its setting (photomontage).

3. FORM EXPLODED

"...and remember that people have peculiar tastes."
Lou Reed.

Heroic Modernism was under the illusion that it could replace the treatises and patterns of "the old architecture" with a new set of prototypes (Le Corbusier's "five points" replacing the column, the pediment and the entablature).

However, the freedom of form in architecture that has been in evidence for the past two decades goes against this hypothesis. It has various possible origins: the exhaustion of traditional symbols, advances in construction techniques, and the exploration of form by artists opening up the possibility of unprecedented inventions... The complex world revealed through the increased availability of images has also played a role in founding the new awareness of a multiplicity of cultures all affirming their identities and their differences.

Once the age old questions of stability and convenience had been resolved, the architect found himself free to give expression to and to reinvent form itself, rather than a language with a fixed, codified vocabulary and grammar. Architecture is coming to terms with a loss of gravity, in both senses of the word.

The following pages illustrate the plethora of forms, some harking back to the avant-gardes of the past, others emerging from some improbable planet, UFOs, lonely, orphaned objects that may well have no posterity. ■

Opposite
Nationale-Nederlanden Office Building
Prague, Czech Republic
Frank O. Gehry

Views of the model.
The corner site of the Nationale-Nederlanden Office Building is adjacent to an unusually shaped public square and calls for a twin tower scheme that makes a smooth transition from one street to the next, while at the same time creating a strong visual focus.
This massing strategy also establishes a sculptural dialogue appropriate to the urban context. The main exterior facade, overlooking the river bank, responds to the rich textures and scale of the adjacent row of houses.

CHRISTIAN DE PORTZAMPARC

Paris, France

Christian de Portzamparc belonged to the May 1968 generation that broke violently with the Beaux-Arts tradition. He was a supporter of the "return to the city" movement and was wary of Modernism in its most dogmatic form. The "Hautes Formes", a housing development in Paris, brought him to the attention of the general public. The buildings that date from the early eighties display a rather rigid formalism which he has left behind in his mature work: the Cité de la Musique at La Villette and the hotel opposite at the Porte de Pantin in Paris prove his loyalty to his urban commitments, the freedom he has acquired with form and his mastery of technique and vision.

Cité de la Musique, Parc de La Villette, Paris, France

The Cité de la Musique is a "suite" in the musical sense, a series of paths, of places that are discovered by wandering through them. "In architecture, as in music, things are perceived in a time sequence, in duration. I am very attached to the fact that architecture should encourage movement: we go from one place to another because we want to discover something." The design of the auditorium permits new relationships between the audience and the musicians, and the optimal use of space for different types of music: symphonic, chamber music, recitals. Colour is of paramount importance throughout the Cité. For example, in the auditorium lighting is provided in the three primary colours which a computer programme can combine into limitless variations. Thus, the auditorium can take on all the colours of the rainbow and the changing colours can be programmed to "play" in sequence.

Crédit Lyonnais Tower, Lille, France

The design for the Crédit Lyonnais tower is the exact solution to an equation with several unknowns: to build a 50 m (55 yds) bridge over the TGV train station with a fixed budget; to rise 120 m (131 yds) into the air at at least one point and yet not exceed 15,000 sq.m. (17,943 sq.yds) in area; to orient the buiding towards the south of the city; and to create for it its own specific form.

Cité de la Musique
Parc de La Villette, Paris, France.

Opposite
Housing, Fukuoka
Japan.

Overleaf
Cité de la Musique
Parc de La Villette, Paris, France.

Above
General view,
Parc de La Villette.
Below
Auditorium.

Extension to the Palais des Congrès, Paris, France

The extension to the Palais des Congrès corresponds to a double aim: to improve the functioning and performance of the existing building and to improve the quality of the site as part of the city. The new facade must therefore be designed to catch the attention of people in passing cars: it has to be clearly defined and simple, immediately accessible but also subtle when viewed over time. Finally, it has to has to serve as a huge notice board to advertize the programme of activities.

Bandaï Cultural Complex, Tokyo, Japan

The Cultural Complex has been designed as a form to receive and diffuse light. By day, the play of changing light and sculptural planes gives the building a strong presence on the avenue. At dusk, a programme of coloured lighting bathes the edifice in a mysterious atmosphere.

Opposite
Crédit Lyonnais Tower
Lille, France.

The orientation of the upper floors passes from north-south to east-west through a progressive deformation of the tower that opens onto the south and the city of Lille.

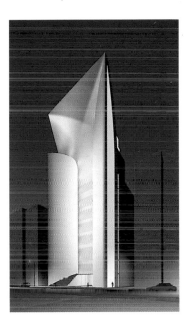

Bandaï Cultural Complex
Tokyo, Japan.
View of the model.

Left
Extension to the Palais des Congrès
Paris, France.

The huge opening in the diagonal plane itself brings light into the entrance and the diagonal functions as a canopy. In this opening a cone symbolizes softness. the outside curves round to become the inside. A horizontal plane cuts through the diagonal plane, serving as an immense support for texts and images, a lectern for the city.

KIYOSHI SEY TAKEYAMA

Osaka, Japan

Kiyoshi Sey Takeyama's aim is to create relationships between incomplete things and events, to give structure to isolated phenomena in a world which is fragmented, discontinuous, and incomplete. His work, often using symbolic ideas, has both solidity and stillness, while at the same time emphasising discontinuity and fragmentation as positive values – because, ultimately, "we have no alternative but to live and act in such a context."

The Future of the City
Essay

The city is a fabric woven from "memories". Architecture is an incubator for time. The technologies that have allowed human life to prosper in the past were methods of time preservation. Books have preserved time for thought. Photographs, recordings, films, videos, have preserved time in various ways by light or sound. In a similar way, works of architecture have materialized the programme of each age, thus presenting time in many different ways. Architecture is a "memory factory".

One of the features of "incomplete form" is its interaction with other forms, like the electron exchanging ions. Another is its capacity for architectural expression which reflects our consciousness. To define the "present", we can only describe it in an incomplete way. The invention of communication technologies has made all sorts of information accessible to us. But these technologies have broken down the information into bits and pieces. Conversely, we could say that society, by adopting fragmentary information, has made it possible for communication technologies to progress rapidly. We no longer dream of a self-sufficient utopia with a common treasury of information. We must seek our own place in the midst of the flood of incomplete, fragmentary, broken bits and pieces of information. At present, and in the future, we can see the world only in terms of a continual discontinuity of incomplete events. The incompleteness of information, and the incompleteness of human existence embody a "present", where various "times" coexist.

The media, which are the products of human invention, have changed our consciousness and given us a new vision of the world. As long as architecture is a representation of our consciousness of space, the architecture that represents the "present" cannot avoid being incomplete. For only in an incomplete form can the future become present.

Shuto-cho Pastoral Hall,
Yamaguchi, Japan.

Opposite
Above
Outside Auditorium.
Below
Inside Auditorium.

Below
Section showing the two auditoriums.

Shuto-cho Pastoral Hall, Yamaguchi, Japan

This Pastoral Hall is designed for the performance of classical music and to be the focal point for cultural activities in the park surrounding it. For Takeyama, architecture is the stylization of the earth and its contours, and although technology has made it possible to rise above the earth's surface, it is still the fundamental meaning and nature of architecture to work with the contours of the planet. An awareness of "creating contours" penetrates the entire design of the park. A promenade has been designed that is not solely the means to an end, but also a process, a place for wandering with no purpose. The contours of the promenade are intended to provoke interaction between those who have come for a specific event and those who are lost in silence, or in music.

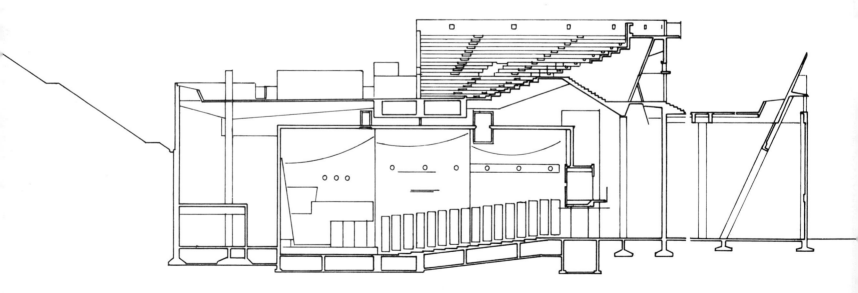

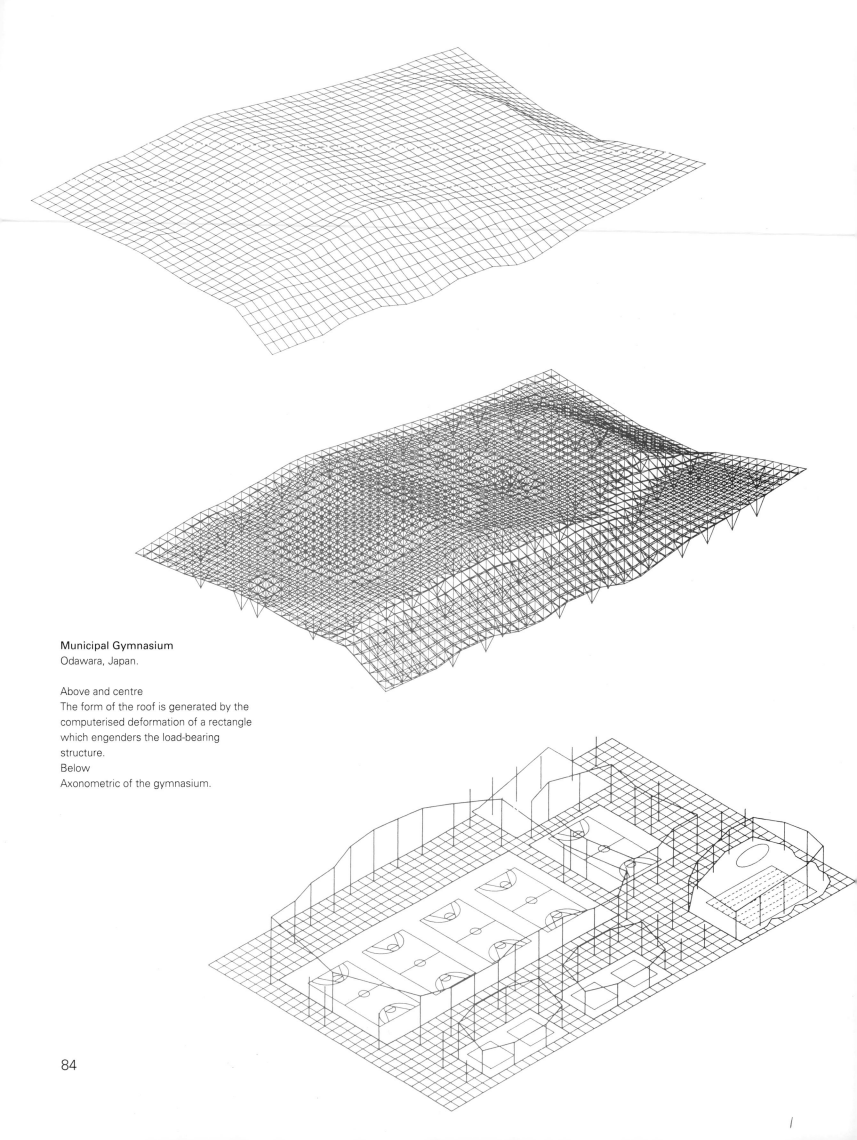

Municipal Gymnasium
Odawara, Japan.

Above and centre
The form of the roof is generated by the computerised deformation of a rectangle which engenders the load-bearing structure.
Below
Axonometric of the gymnasium.

SHOEI YOH

Fukuoka, Japan

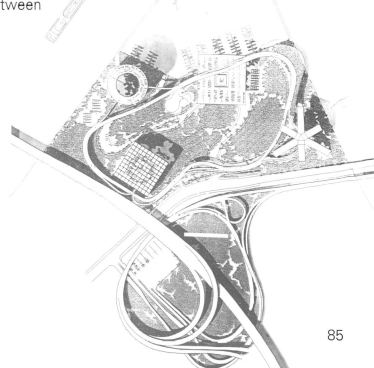

Aerial City
Daïkoku Pier, Yokohama, Japan.

Below and overleaf
Views of the model.

Four objects - a cube, a cylinder, an upside-down pyramid and a tripod - are linked by an overhead motorway network, leaving the ground free.

A brilliant student, Shoei Yoh graduated from the University of Keio Gijuku in Tokyo at the age of twenty-two and then studied art in the United States before setting up his architectural practice in Fukuoka in 1970.

His reputation was made by two spectacular yet subtle projects: the "trellis of light" house (1980) and the "sun clock" house. Both houses rest on a simple premise: a geometrical envelope – a simple parallelepiped – is broken up by thin glazed slits, creating an orthogonal grid. In this way, the sun casts a pattern of light and shade over the ground and walls that moves with the progress of the day. By night, internal light sources redefine the volumes of the house. Since the early 1990s, Shoei Yoh's preoccupations have extended to include more general (and, in Japan, more urgent) problems, those of land use and the distribution of natural and urban environments.

Aerial City, Yokohama, Japan

The Daikoku Pier at Aerial City, Yokohama, is an example of ecological land use in the context of a high-rise city. Daikoku Pier is a road 5 m (5 1/2 yds) above the ground with colossal curves that are destined to change the appearance of the whole city.

Masterplan showing the motorway network.

Once the city has been built, all roads, streets and traffic lights will disappear, and the natural environment will once again reemerge at ground level, thus creating an extremely convenient, highly efficient, 24-hour-a-day city rising over green, shady woods. Then the choice between city and country will belong to the past.

Municipal Gymnasium, Odawara, Japan

For Shoei Yoh, the Municipal Gymnasium in Odawara is an example of what he calls "aquatic architecture". This is a more fluid and open system of urban space made possible by new technologies, in particular, by computer-assisted methods of design.

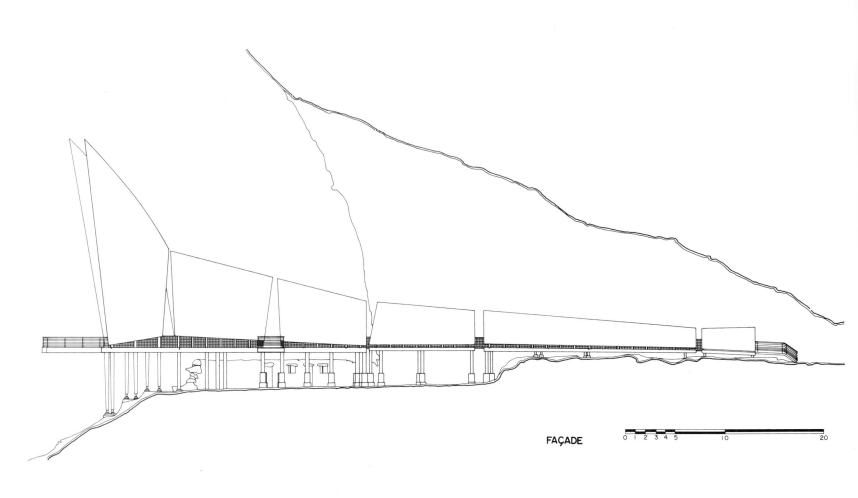

FAÇADE

0 1 2 3 4 5   10   20

MASSIMILIANO FUKSAS

Rome, Italy
Paris, France

Shortly before graduating, Massimiliano Fuksas played a leading role in the May 1968 events in Rome. His work as an architect has the same provocative eloquence that characterized his political activity. His first practice was in Rome, where he created several pieces of virtuoso anarchy in neighbouring towns, buildings that appeared both disordered and unbalanced (the gymnasium in Paliano in 1985, the cemetery for Civita Castellana in 1989). During the 1980s, France too benefitted from his euphioric activism, as he produced buildings which were both sensitive to place and out-of-phase with standard expectations (the Maison de la Confluence in 1989, the mediatheque at Rézé in 1991). His early work was characterized by expressive figuration on an extravagant scale, but he now seems to be moving towards a kind of austerity that is more conceptual than formal.

Graffiti Museum, entrance to the Niaux caves, Ariège, France

The entrance to the Niaux caves enhances the site and at the same time signals its importance. The concept is based on a sort of large, prehistoric animal, coming out of the caves, its wings open to welcome the visitors. It is conceived as part of the archaeology of the site, and this impression is reinforced by the rusted steel used for its construction.

Candie Saint-Bernard, Paris, France

The renovation of the Candie Saint-Bernard district of Paris is Massimiliano Fuksas's first commission in the city. It is part of a larger scheme for the renovation of a typical working-class district, the faubourg Saint-Antoine. Fuksas already knew the district well: he had made a proposal for the redevelopment of the old railway line leading to the Bastille. He was therefore familiar with the dense 19th-century buildings penetrated only by passage-ways and dead-ends leading under porches. The problem was twofold: the gymnasium needed to be visible so as to attract people, but at the same time the somewhat old-fashioned charm of the neighbourhood had to be preserved.

Fuksas sited the various elements of the programme according to the simplest and most effective rules for urban planning: the tennis court and gymnasium are aligned on an east-west axis; housing and shops recompose the facade of the rue Charles-Delescluze in line with the existing buildings.

In order to articulate the general shape of the development, Fuksas uses one of his most familiar devices, an ironic metaphor – a computer printer churning out a continuous ream of paper in three distinct waves: the first covers the entrance and service areas of the gymnasium; the other two, linked by bridges,

Candie Saint-Bernard
Paris, France.

Right
Gymnasium

Below
View of the housing.

Opposite
Above
West elevation.
Below
View of the zinc facades.

provide housing, with the added benefit that some apartments straddle the two waves and can thus make use of two levels staggered to the west.

The incongruous forms that make the whole complex seem out-of-scale are domesticated by the traditional zinc of roofs and facades and their regular openings.

For the gymnasium and the sports facilities, the materials and colours chosen are harsh: rough concrete, grey and black textures. The result is aesthetically brutal and direct, but tempered by sensitive details and by the freshness of the black and white fresco by Enzo Cucchi.

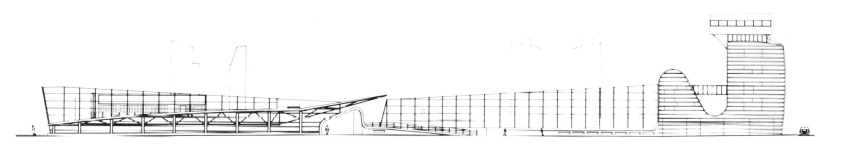

ODILE DECQ AND BENOÎT CORNETTE

Paris, France

Odile Decq and Benoît Cornette first came to public notice with their work for the Bank of Brittany in Rennes (1990). Since then, their reputation has grown as practitioners of a dynamic, metallic architecture, clearly inspired by the punk movement. Their projects emphasize movement, three-dimensionality and asymmetry in opposition to monumental stasis, frontal presentation and symmetry. Their aesthetic is kinetic, even cinematic, in the way in which it plays with ideas of speed and procession.

Carrières-sur-Seine Viaduct and
Motorway Control Station, Nanterre, France

On the one hand, a viaduct that links an underground junction and a motorway bridge; on the other, a building: the control station for the motorway network. Above, the motorway with its noise, its speed, the smell of petrol; below, a landscaped park along the Seine, the end of the green corridor that runs along the historical axis of Paris. Between the two, a pilot building. Located in a network of flows and fluidity, this project is a place of passage with its own dynamic equilibrium.

The three main elements of the viaduct, the roadway, supports and piers are clearly disassociated from one another. Thus, the functional autonomy and the structural role of each of the elements are clearly identifiable and the construction's appearance is considerably simplified. The continuity of the park is thus preserved and the green area is not imprisoned within a wall of motorway.

Better still, the position of the control station also preserves the physical continuity of the park.

Rather than placing the control station like a barrier in the middle of the park, it has been raised off the ground and attached to the underside of the motorway bridge. The area under the building is no more than a shadow on the green park. Thanks to this miracle of levitation, the control station in no way forms part of the park, but clearly belongs to the motorway system, of which it constitutes the pilot's cabin.

But the control station is submarine as well as air-borne. It is immersed in the flow of traffic that continuously rushes past. Only the supervisor's box protrudes. This volume is inserted between the two roadways that make up the motorway bridge, rising above the traffic with its antenna raised towards the sky, thus marking the entrance to the capital and the nerve centre of the motorway control system.

93

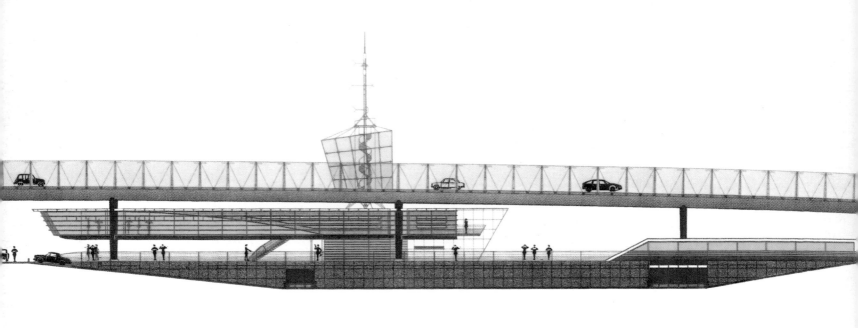

Motorway Control Station
Nanterre, France.

Above
Elevation.
Centre
Cross section.
Below
General plan.

Opposite
Colour perspective.

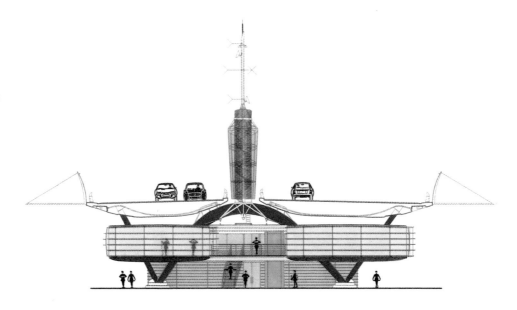

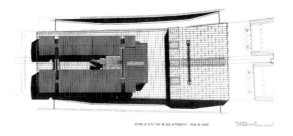

GÜNTHER DOMENIG

Graz, Austria

Günther Domenig began by flirting with the ideas of megastructure that were fashionable in the 1960s. He went on to play an active part in the school of young Austrian architects known as the School of Graz. An office building that appeared to be the result of a catastrophe, a high-tech masterpiece that had passed through an earthquake – the Central Savings Bank in Vienna (1979) – sealed his reputation.

Domenig has set out to explore new territory for expressionism. His menacing figures in concrete and steel evoke Atlantic bunkers or the space ship of the film *Alien*. They make a strong and unsettling statement.

Opposite and overleaf
Stone House
Steindorf, Austria.
General views.

Stone House, Steindorf, Autriche

Architecture and landscape
Architecture and the site
Architecture and the idea
The one site
grass and stone
The other site
open and soft
The subjective dimensions of the site
The site as memory
The site as experience
The site as representation
The site as self-representation

Hills rise from the ground
rocks burst through
They are separated by an abyss
The rocks are metal
and the hills are walls
Spaces and paths
leading below the water table

cut through them.
Deep down in the basement
the spiral staircase
the arrow
and water emerging from the ground
in the stationary
and in the floating
rocks dreams also
come piggy-back
The abyss is where one walks
the cube where one meets
the wedge where one eats.
The low path under the water
to the water
the high path
to the water
and into the water
Breaking out
getting ready
to break through

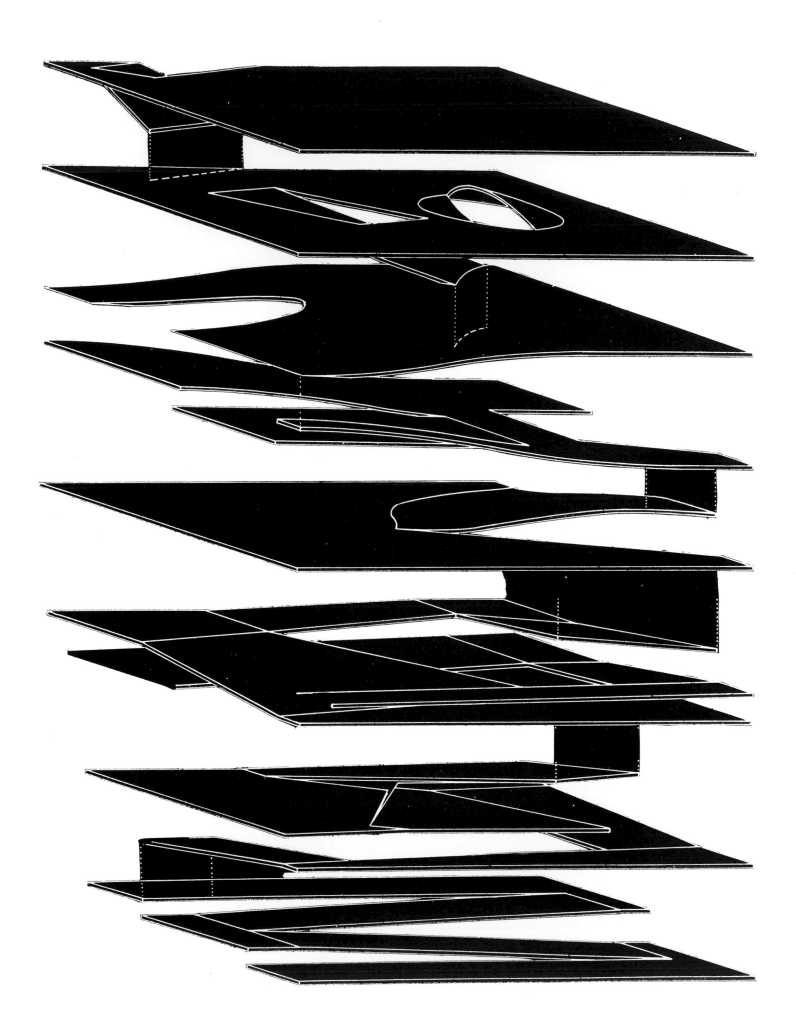

OMA – REM KOOLHAAS

Rotterdam, Netherlands

Rem Koolhaas and OMA (Office for Metropolitan Architecture) established their reputation in the 1970s through a series of provocative manifesto-projects, culminating in a book which proclaimed the need for a "culture of congestion": *New York Delirium*.

These projects were inspired by the determination to return to a modernity that had somehow managed to survive on the other side of the Atlantic, thanks to an overwhelming culture of optimism. "The richest ideas are to be found lying in the dustbin of history", Koolhaas said later. "If there is a method to be employed in this work [architecture], then it is that of systematic idealization, the automatic over-estimation of the existing state of affairs, a speculative onslaught which [...] will be unleashed even on what is most mediocre".

Rem Koolhaas's talents are obvious in his dance theatre in The Hague, the Alva house, the Rotterdam Kunsthalle and the Lille Conference Centre. His next great challenge will be the libraries for the Jussieu university campus in Paris, for which he won the competition in 1992.

The Two Libraries, Jussieu campus, Paris, France

The Jussieu libraries will not be a building, but a network. Conceived at the hub of the campus, they will gather there like a residue, plain, empty, sandwiched between their base and the existing buildings.

So as to make its presence felt again, we have imagined in this project that the surface of the ground area is flexible, a sort of communal flying carpet, which we have folded up to create a pile of platforms. These platforms will complete the grid patterns of the Jussieu site.

The essential problem of the present gound plan is its dispersion. By reconfiguring it in this way, its substance can be concentrated. So as to take best advantage of the site, the two libraries will be situated according to a relationship that is "inversely proportional" to the platforms and the reading rooms. Thus, the science library will be underground, while the humanities library will rise above the plaza which leads to the metro station to the south and to the river Seine to the north. The plaza will advance into the building like a double helix to form the reception area.

Instead of simply piling up levels one on top of the other, the planes of each floor will be modified to connect them both to the floor above and the floor below. Thus a continuous path leads through the whole building, like the loops of an interior boulevard, offering both access and visibility. The visitor is like Baudelaire's *flâneur*, an observer who is seduced by the world of books, information and "urban situations" through which he strolls.

Opposite
The Two Libraries, Jussieu
Paris, France.
The form is a pile of platforms that are cut out and unfolded in a continuous strip.

The Two Libraries, Jussieu,
Paris, France.

Above
North facade (facing the Seine), east facade
(facing the Jardin des Plantes), south
facade (facing the Jussieu campus) and
west facade (facing the Institute of the
Arab World).
Below
Sections.

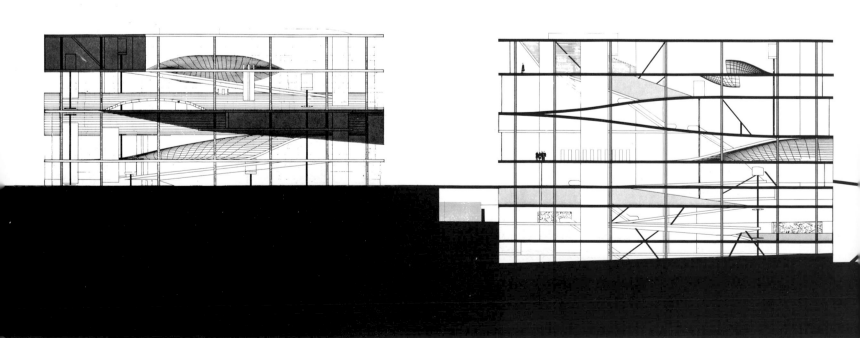

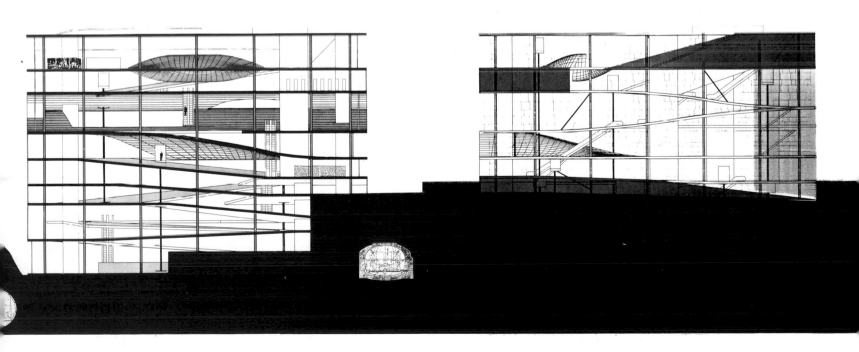

The Two Libraries, Jussieu campus
Paris, France.

Above
Interiors (studies).
Above right
Structural model.
Below
Unfolded section and level plans
with circulation paths.

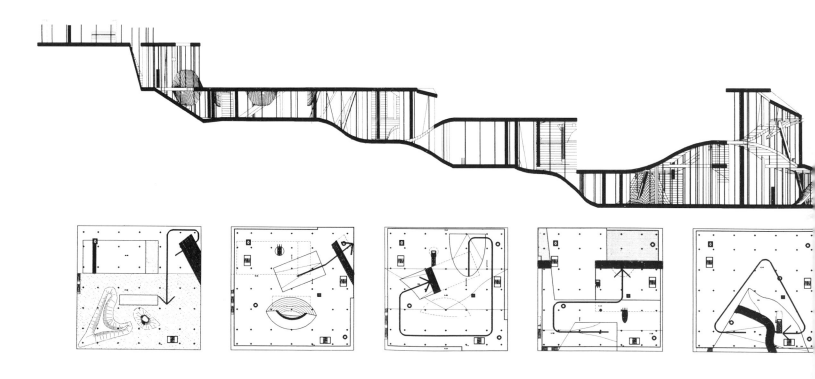

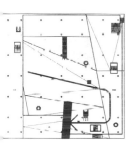  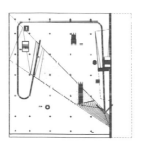 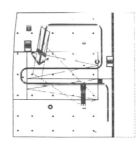 

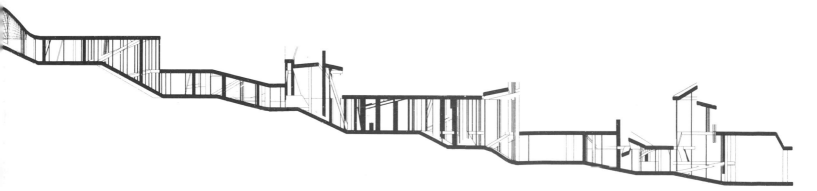

ZAHA HADID

London, Great Britain

Zaha Hadid comes from Irak, but has long made her home in London, where she graduated from the Architectural Association*. She first came to public notice with OMA in 1978, for her entry in the competition for the parliament building in The Hague. Her earliest projects were influenced by Malevich and Supremacism, and she has retained her taste for a weightless architecture, created by displacing large plane surfaces in an ethereal space. Her winning project in the 1983 competition for "The Peak" in Hong Kong was exemplary in this respect. She has disarmed envious critics with the success of her built projects – in Japan, or near Basle, with the fire station she designed for the furniture manufacturer and architecture "collector", Vitra. It is no longer possible to cast doubt on the appropriacy of her methods and the spatial wealth of her painterly designs.

Art and Media Centre, Düsseldorf, Germany

The Düsseldorf Art and Media Centre project provided the impetus for the redevelopment of the old Düsseldorf harbour area. Rising from the river, an enormous metallic triangle pierces the wall, to form an entrance ramp to the street and a sloping plaza below. The adjoining ground planes crack open to reveal technical studios to the north, shops and restaurants to the south. Below ground, the technical service aeras are compressed into a wall part of which rises above ground, curving round to form a 320-seat cinema. On the street side the wall has tiny, linear incisions in its concrete elevation; while on the river side, individual floors are articulated by varying depths of cantilever. One floor breaks completely free, leaving a void which becomes a terrace; then, on reaching an adjoining block, it turns into a solid black box.

The advertising agency is an even more fragmented series of slabs, set perpendicular to the street. It is a minimalist glass box surrounded by a family of sculptured supports and heavy, triangular, transfer structures.

Vitra Fire Station, Weil am Rhein, Germany

The whole building is petrified movement, expressing the tension of being on the alert all the time, and the potential to burst into action at any moment. The walls seem to slide past each other, while the large sliding doors literally form a moving wall.

The fire station also functions as a screening device in front of neighbouring buildings, thus complicating the identity of the Vitra complex. Space-defining and screening functions were the point of departure for the

107

architectural concept: a linear, layered series of walls. The activities of the fire station occupy the spaces between these walls, which open, tilt on break in two, according to functional requirements.

Cardiff Bay Opera House, Cardiff, Great Britain

The building concept of the Cardiff Bay Opera House is based on the architectural expression of the hierarchy between serviced and servicing spaces: the auditorium and the other public and semi-public performance and rehearsal spaces are threaded like jewels on a string of rationally aligned support accommodation. This band is then wrapped around the perimeter of the site like an inverted necklace where all the jewels turn towards each other, creating a concentrated public space between them, accessible to the public from the centre, while serviced from the back around the perimeter.

Vitra Fire Station
Weil am Rhein, Germany.

Opposite
Above
The exterior at night.
Below
Interior.

Below
Concept drawing.

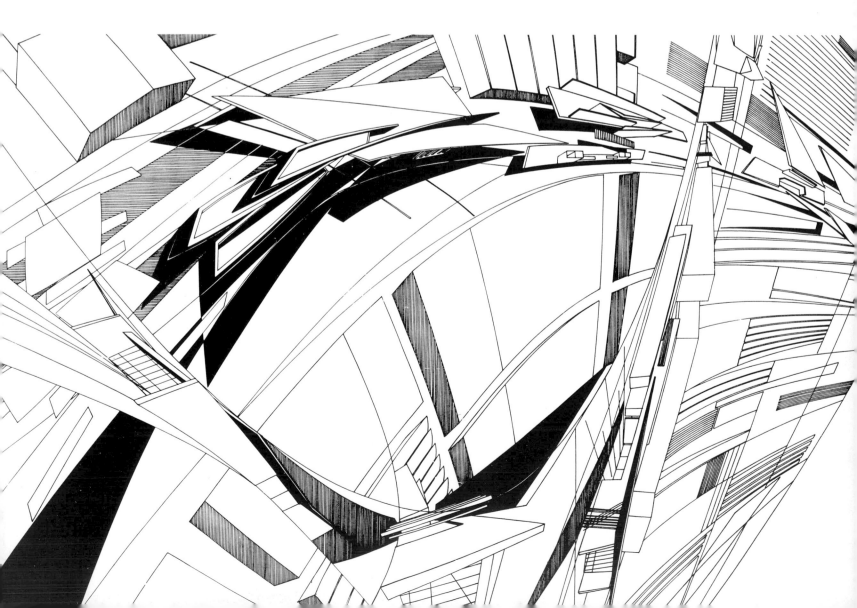

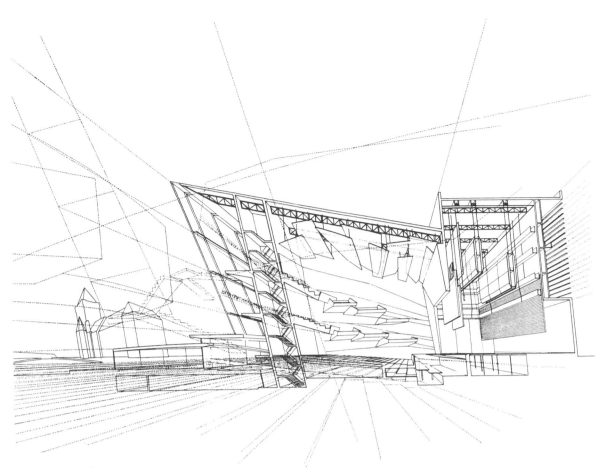

Cardiff Bay Opera House
Cardiff,
Great Britain.

Above
Section.
Below
View of the model.

Opposite

Above
Overall plan
Below
Aerial view of the second
model.

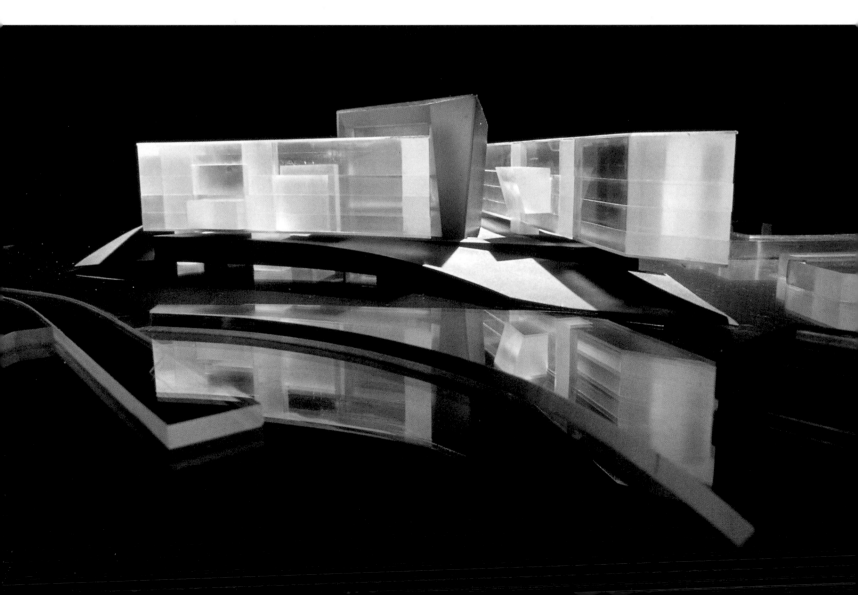

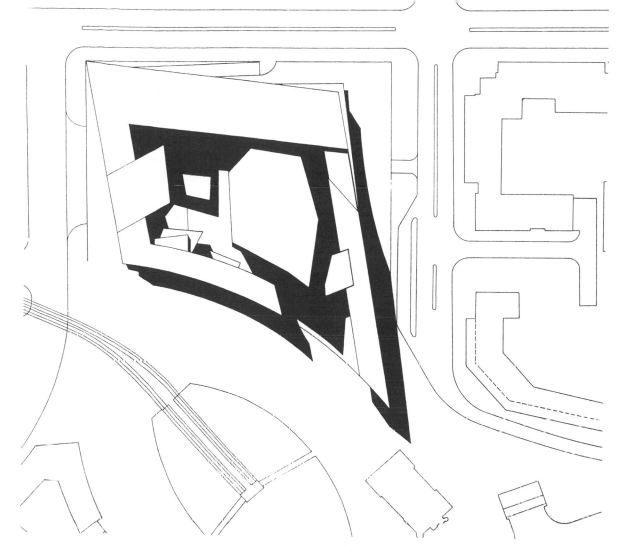

COOP HIMMELBLAU

Vienna, Austria
Los Angeles, California, USA

In the late 1960s, Vienna was suddenly invaded by psychedelic space capsules, giant inflatables and self-sufficient bubbles, a participative, subversive, pneumatic and hedonistic architecture that, once again, was destined to change our lives. The main protagonists in this adventure were Missing Link*, Haus Rucker Co* and Coop Himmelblau.

Once these dreams of a spatial Eden had evaporated, Coop Himmelblau recentred their activities on developing a provocative and abrasive architectural style. Their aim is weightlessness, and their means are the inversion of the interior/exterior distinction. But all their taut cables and protruding antennae cannot entirely hide their highly sophisticated technical achievements.

A Future of Splendid Desolation
Essay

The architectures of the future have already been built.

The solitude of its squares, the desolation of its streets, the devastation of its buildings characterize the city of the present and will characterize the city of the future as well. Expressions like "safe and sound" are no longer applicable to architecture.

We live in a world of unloved objects, relics of an urban civilisation. We have these objects, and we use them daily to our advantage. Today's architecture reinforces this discrepancy, until it becomes schizophrenic.

Reactionary architecture tends to conceal the problems rather than create the necessary new urban awareness.

Today's architecture must be defined as a medium of expanding vitality.

Contemporary architecture will be honest and true, when streets, open spaces, buildings and infrastructures reflect the image of urban reality, when the devastation of the city is transformed into fascinating landmarks of desolation. Desolation not as a result of complacency but as a result of the identification of urban reality will encourage the desires, the self-confidence and the courage necessary to take hold of the city and to alter it.

The important thing won't then be the grass you can't walk on, but the asphalt you can.

Of course, you will have to discard everything that may obstruct this "emotional act of using". The false aesthetic, which sticks like smeared make-up to the face of mediocrity, the cowardice of antiquated values, the belief that everything that is disquieting can be beautified. The autocrats whose motto is "efficiency, economy and expediency".

Opposite
UFA Cinema Complex
Dresden, Germany.
The building typology forms a spatial
sequence leading from a triangular volume
(UFA Cinema Centre) to a cylinder
(existing UFA cinema palace) to a slab
and a rectangular volume.

Architects must stop thinking only of how to accommodate their clients.
Architects have to stop pitying themselves for the bad company they keep.
Architecture is not a means to an end.
Architecture does not have to function.
Architecture is not palliative. It is the bone in the meat of the city.
Architecture gains meaning in proportion to its desolation.
This desolation comes from the act of using, it gains strength from the surrounding desolation.
And this architecture brings the message:
Everything you like is bad.
Everything that works is bad.
Whatever has to be accepted is good.

UFA Cinema Complex, Dresden, Germany

The UFA Cinema Complex unites three districts of Dresden into one continuous urban landscape. Its triangular form is seen as a transparent glass envelope which, like an aquarium, houses a liquid space filled with free-floating, dynamic entities. The external facades are made up of multiple screens through which the people inside can be seen moving around amid changing patterns of light and colour.

The Groningen Museum, Netherlands

The design concept for the new Groningen Museum of Art is based on the idea of unfolding positive and negative space. The section mass evokes a series of broken volumes with the different strata revealed along the sectional lines. The breaks in the skin allow the inside to come out as well as the outside to fold inwards. The building has been described as volumes placed in a light-space, volumes of light cutting through mass.

UFA Cinema Complex
Dresden, Germany.

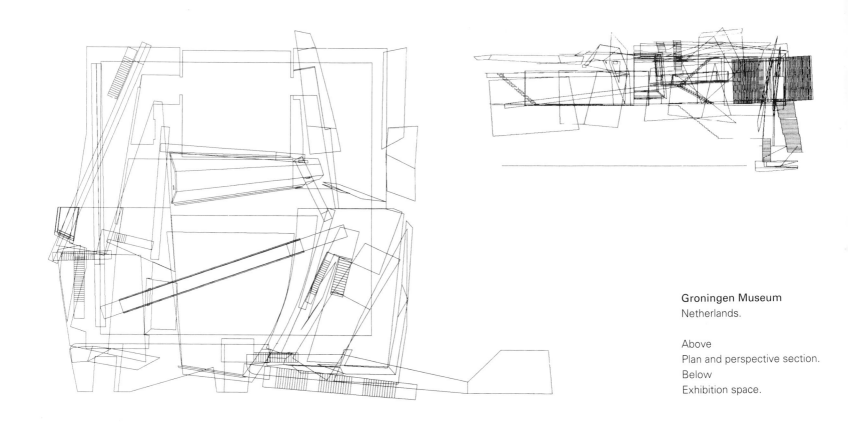

Groningen Museum
Netherlands.

Above
Plan and perspective section.
Below
Exhibition space.

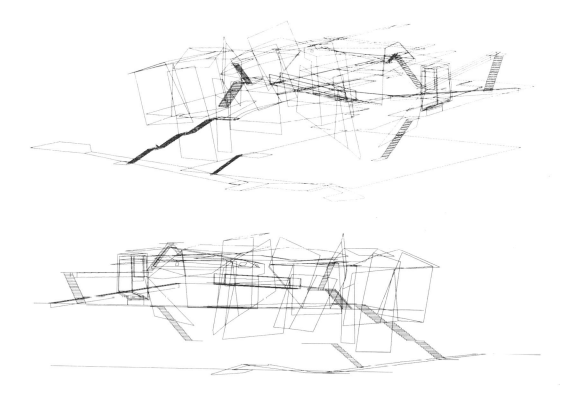

Above
Computer-assisted perspective sections.
Below
Exhibition space.

Overleaf
South-west facade.

ENRIC MIRALLES MOYA

Barcelona, Spain

Enric Miralles has been at the forefront of the new wave of contemporary Spanish architecture which combines the rigour and restraint of the modernist tradition with formal invention, material sensuality and contextual sensitivity. His work seems to break down the barriers between architecture and landscape, so that the man-made and the natural gradually merge and fuse.

New Entrance to Takaoka Railway Station, Japan

The aim of the new entrance is to articulate the way to the station by creating a landmark at the end of the avenue leading to it, and to restore to the square in front of the station the symmetry that was destroyed by a traffic layout that ignored all design and planning criteria. The architect describes his preoccupations as follows:

"The road leads to a square... The necessity of information... Trains and services... We wanted a facade which would take into account all the light and all the urban elements of a railway station complex... Communication links, display boards, wires, rails... As well as roofed-over areas where you can buy tickets or wait for the bus, safe from the weather."

Meditation Pavilion, Unazaki Gorge, Japan

The Meditation Pavilion in the Gorge of Unazaki was designed to make a traditional excursion spot even more attractive. A bridge, a small park and an old pilgrims' path have been linked to form an ensemble that is at one with the rugged beauty of nature.

"The snow which collects in the hollows will form artificial mountains and, later on, small fast-flowing streams of rain water... The transparent surfaces will mirror the contours of the mountains, the water of the river, the fish and the birds..."

Opposite
New Entrance to Takaoka Station
Japan.

The perspective of the new station entrance creates a focal point at the end of the avenue. It consists of lightweight elements, columns and rails, with electronic displays, showing all the necessary information for travellers. Groups of aluminium rails bearing the illuminated lettering run along the facade. They are supported by columns of concrete and steel. In front of the entrance, the columns draw close to form a forest. Some of them pierce through the roofs which are covered with metal or glass.

Perspective of the structure of the rails.

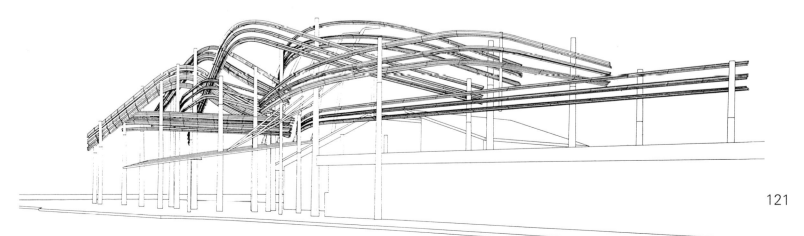

Meditation Pavilion
Unazaki Gorge, Japan.

Above
Overall plan.

Opposite and below
View of the pavilion.

The pavilion is anchored in the steep mountain slope and hangs out over the abyss, supported by pillars arranged in pairs. The frame consists of steel girders and is filled in with glass and wooden panels. Steel frames, covered with bamboo shoots, form a screen, creating a feeling of intimacy. The roof in glass and zinc sheeting consists of a number of elements set off against one another at different angles and in varying shapes and materials. Design criteria were:
Search for the best location for the pavilion.
Establishment of the best route for travellers.
Exploring the scenic landscape.
Architecture as the preparation for a moment of meditation and inner peace, of fusion with an almost virgin landscape.
Showing due respect by careful analysis of the genius loci.
Exploring every turn in the path.
Understanding the gigantic changes in scale which the bridge introduces into the landscape.

FRANKLIN D. ISRAEL

Los Angeles, California, USA

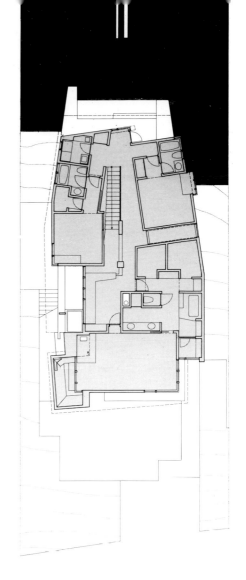

Born in New York, Frank Israel studied at Yale and Columbia, winning the 1973 Rome Prize. His early life was nomadic, as he moved between a period at the American Academy in Rome, and his position as a "senior" architect with Llewelin-Davies, the agency that was responsible for the major urban development projects of the Shah of Iran. In 1977, "exiled from his own town", it was almost inevitable Israel should settle in Los Angeles. There he taught, was involved in the cinema and, under the influence of Frank Gehry, returned to architectural practice. His work since then has played on the sensuality of materials and colours (in an Angelino tradition closer to Schindler than to Neutra), composing object landscapes, micro-cities that fluctuate between tension and relaxation.

Drager House, Berkeley, California, USA

The Drager House replaces the original 1926 house which was destroyed by forest fires in 1991. The new design takes full advantage of the topography of the site, whether backing onto the existing slope of the hill or hollowing it out. Its volume is more modest than that of its predecessor, but the surface area created is greater. The articulation of the different levels is emphasized by terraces and external staircases. Frank Israel here demonstrates his sensitivity to place, giving his own free interpretation of the San Francisco Bay vernacular style. Instead of the omnipresent natural shingle, he uses a copper substitute to enwrap the taut volumes in a willful structure of trapezoid planes, that serve to shade the extensive areas of glazing.

Weisman Pavilion, Brentwood, California, USA

In spite of his many donations in recent years, Frederick Weisman still owns an important collection of contemporary art which his house was no longer large enough to exhibit. So he decided to house it in a new pavilion designed by Frank Israel, a simple structure on two levels built into the hillside.

The lower level, which is accessed from the garden under a porch that also forms a balcony for the gallery, contains the storerooms and studios. The upper level comprises a tall rectangular gallery with a sloping roof, its wooden structure being fully visible.

Two small masterpieces by craftsmen contribute to the effect of this understated building: the porch/balcony that rises up out of the garden facade like some spaceship invented by Jules Verne, and the staircase in wood and metal that leads to the garden from the gallery.

Drager House
Berkeley, California, USA.

Above
Third floor plan.

Opposite
From the south-west.

Below
By night.

Weisman Pavilion
Brentwood, California, USA.

Opposite
The porch/balcony.

Above
Garden facade.
Below
The gallery and the staircase
leading to the garden.

ERIC OWEN MOSS

Los Angeles, California, USA

Born in Los Angeles, Eric Owen Morris was educated at the University of Southern California (UCLA), then made a detour via Berkeley and Harvard, before returning to set up his practice in his home town. Like Frank Gehry, he is acutely sensitive to the specificities of Los Angeles – its loose structure, its contextual vagaries, its heterogeneity of materials. But that is as far as the comparison goes. Frank Gehry's interpretation of this incomplete city is relaxed, not to say disenchanted. But for Moss, the quality-free environment of the suburbs is an exceptional catalyst. He deploys banal, even incongruous materials (chipboard, vitrified clay tubing) with a maniacal precision to create complex geometrics and superbly refined forms.

Samitaur 1, Culver City, California, USA

The building site for Samitaur I is subject to multiple zoning regulations: it's cut off at the top by a height limit; at the bottom by a truck clearance requirement; at the perimeter by the City Fire Department who wouldn't allow the new building above to extend over existing buildings. So the zoning rules defined the limits of an orthogonal block, within which the architect provided certain anomalies, in the form of voids in the block.

There are two primary anomalies, where trucks and cars enter the road under the structure, and where they exit. A conference space and a lounge/bathroom area also constitute exceptions within the block. New steel legs dance around old roll-up doors, while driveways and windows allow existing buildings to operate as before.

Samitaur 1
Culver City, California, USA.
Detail of the model

Opposite
Two views of the model.
The office space is supported on steel legs that straddle the road.

Below
Axonometric.

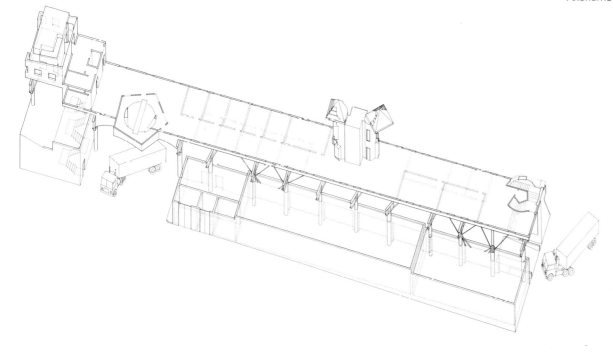

The Box
Culver City, California, USA.

Right
Plans of staircases, the conference room
and the roof .

Opposite
Axonometric.

The Box – reception/deck/conference area –
is one material and one colour, an almost
black cement plaster inside and out. No
material distinctions are made from roof to
wall and none from inside surface to
outside. The Box has three parts. The first is
an almost cylindrical reception area, which
cuts into the roof of the existing wood shed.
Behind the reception area is an exterior stair
that leads to a second level roof deck
supported on the exposed trussed system
below, and suspended over the cylinder.
The zone between square deck and round
roof cut is glazed, lighting the reception
space below. Up the exterior stair, a door
between levels 2 and 3 connects an interior
stair to the Box itself, a private third-floor
conference space.

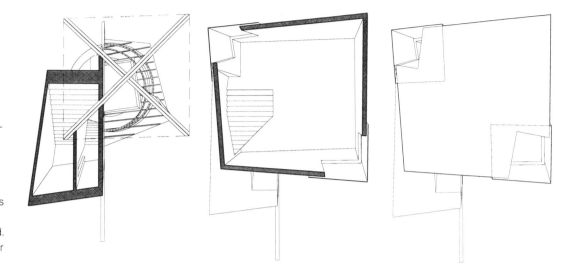

The Box, Culver City, California, USA

The formal expression of the Box – a private third-floor conference space
added to an existing building – works by arguing with the simple, orthogonal
box shape, both as a traditional precept, and as an amended object which
extends the box idea.

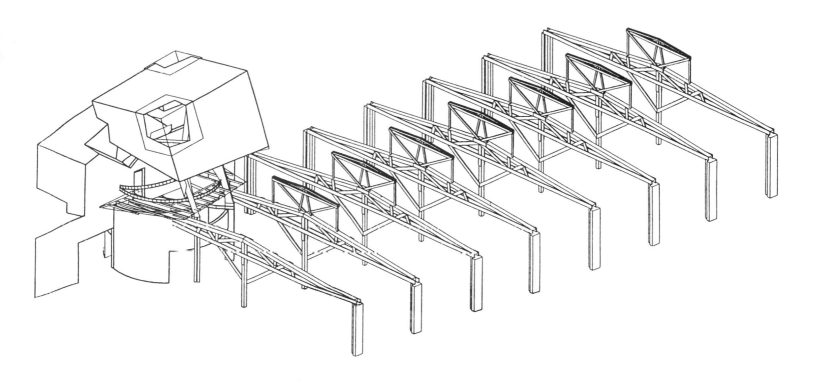

FRANK O. GEHRY

Los Angeles, California, USA

Frank Gehry is an insatiable exporer of the forms and materials available to the contemporary architect. Since the early 1970s, he has been producing work that is strong, proteiform, open to new inventions. His first Angelino constructions – the Ron Davis studio (1972), the Gehry house (1978) – are remarkable for their economy of means, their casting against type of materials, their relaxed execution, their simple yet often skewed geometry and their dramatic perspectives. In his more complex large-scale projects, he uses fragmentation to break up any single sense of scale, and produce an accretion of "small one-room buildings", as at the Loyola Law Faculty in Los Angeles.

His international reputation brought him to Europe, where he built an almost expressionistic museum for Vitra on the outskirts of Basle. The Frederick Weisman Museum in Minneapolis marks a turning point in his work, which Gehry himself has likened to Matisse's discovery of paper cut-outs.

Weisman Art Museum, Minneapolis, USA

The University of Minnesota Museum is intended to draw together a campus that spreads along both banks of the river Mississippi. It is located at one end of the Washington Avenue road bridge, to which it is directly connected by a pedestrian ramp.

The museum space follows a logical sequence: on the main floor, entered from the foot bridge, are the galleries, the auditorium and the permanent collections; beneath them are the service areas, studios and car park; while the "tower" that rises above the galeries houses the administrative offices.

Gehry is always passionate in his attention to light, mixing artificial and natural sources. Here, the natural light comes from three "chimneys" which have been sited to ensure that no ray of light should ever directly strike the picture rails. Whence the turbulent outlines of the building's external form, whose chaos is emphasized by the large plates of bright stainless steel which look out towards the far bank of the river.

Guggenheim Museum, Bilbao, Spain

The Guggenheim Museum in Bilbao is intended to fit in with the existing proportions of the town, and with the traditional construction materials to be found along the river front. The sculptural form of the roof serves to unify the different buildings. The impressive scale of the central atrium allows it to house monumental installations and spectacular one-off events. Equipped with a powerful computer network, the museum is ready to cope with innovations in electronic art forms and performances using the new media.

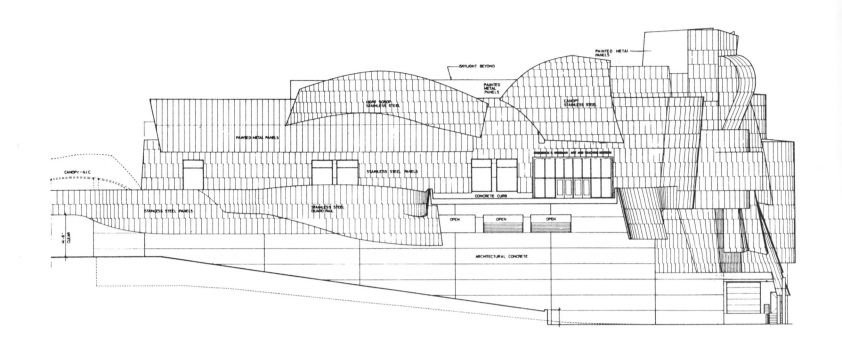

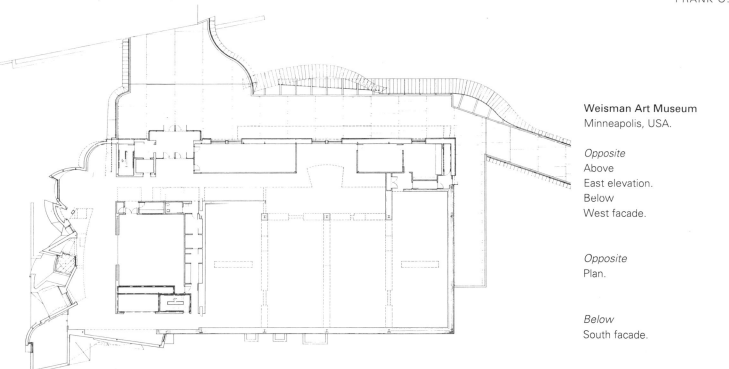

Weisman Art Museum
Minneapolis, USA.

Opposite
Above
East elevation.
Below
West facade.

Opposite
Plan.

Below
South facade.

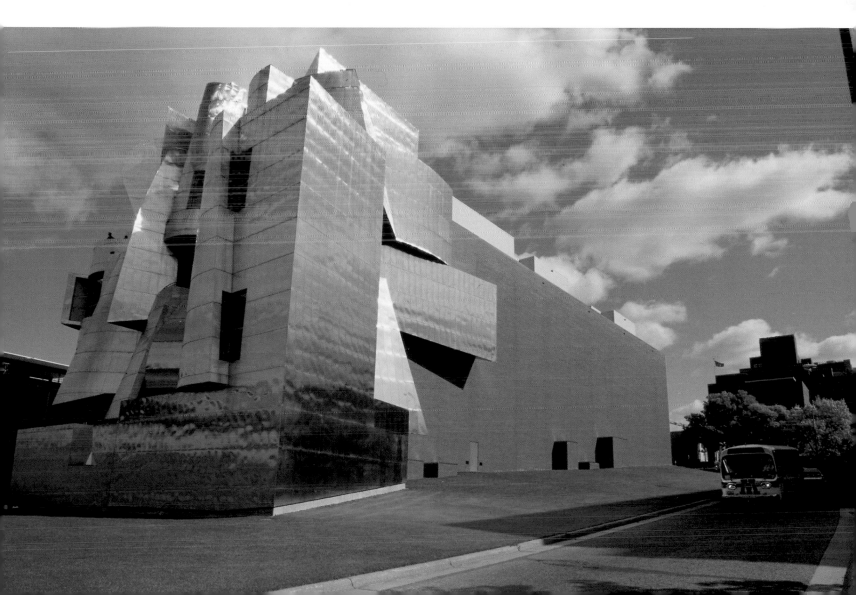

Guggenheim Museum
Bilbao, Spain.

Above
Roof plan.

Below
View of the river facade.

Opposite
Above
Ground floor plan.
Below
General view of the model.

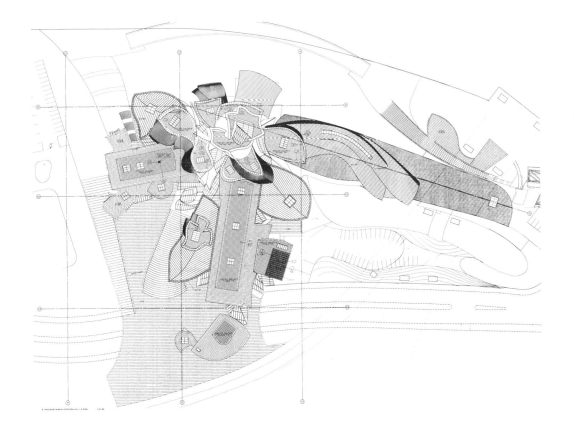

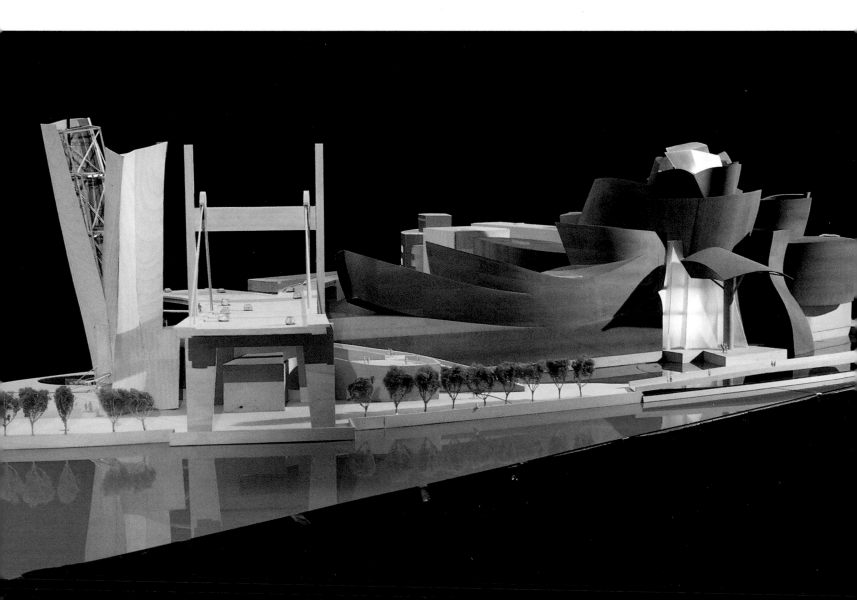

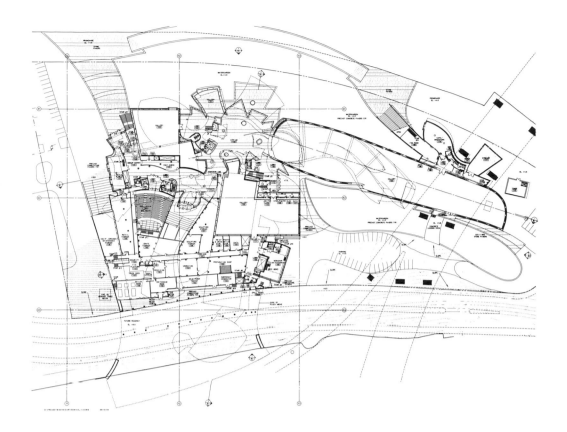

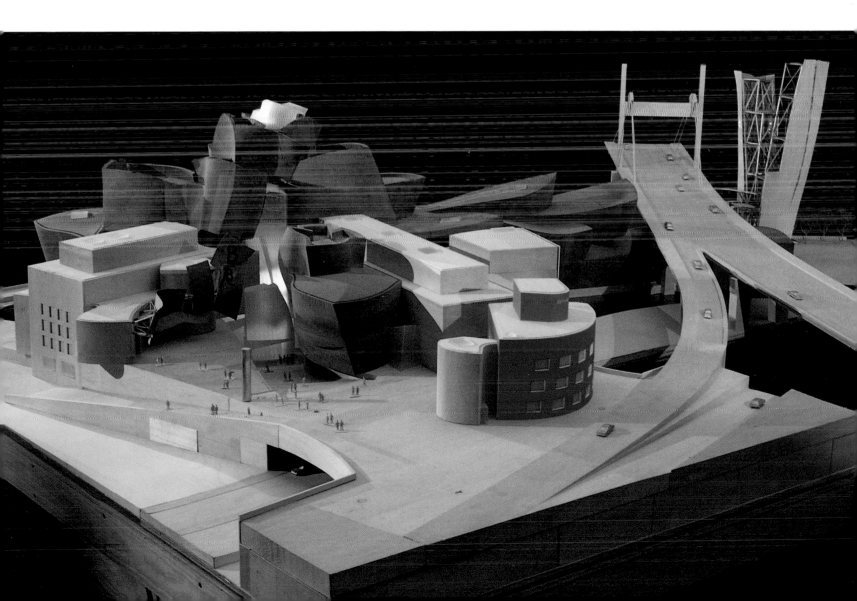

4. A SECOND NATURE

"You know, I think we should put mountains here.
Otherwise, where will the people fall from?
And what if we add a staircase?
Yodellayheehoo."
Laurie Anderson

Ever since the Enlightenment, the loss of nature has haunted the city dweller's conscience. The cruelty and dangers of nature have been forgotten in favour of an idyllic and harmonious image, of nostalgia for a lost paradise or a rediscovered Arcadia based on a new peaceful relationship between man and the elements.

At the end of the 20th century, urbanisation has reawoken this consciousness. For the architect, who deals with the real world, these rejuvenated preoccupations with ecology have taken on a pragmatic form that expresses itself in two opposing ways:

either by restoring the relationship between nature and the human environment that has been compromised: we introduce nature into the city;

– or by questioning the true nature of nature (and thus of artifice) in the light of the questions posed by the apostles of "virtual reality". "After all" Itsuko Hasegawa has said, "all artefacts produced by man have their origin in nature." ∎

Opposite
Atelier at Tomigaya
Japan.
Itsuko Hasegawa

139

EMILIO AMBASZ

New York, USA

Well-known both as a product designer and as an architect, Emilio Ambasz's distinctive approach stems from his special interest in the nature of materials and his reinterpretation of natural environments through technology. His tendency to design series of highly-defined, technologically sophisticated objects connected to each other by a narrative thread, points to the influence of his work as a product designer. But his characteristic explorations of the ground plane as a three-dimensional space in itself are specifically architectural.

Opposite
House for Leo Castelli

Green cities: ecology and architecture
Essay

A green town is man-created architecture that is in harmony with nature and the earth to provide a friendly space for human beings. There is a great tradition in urban planning, starting in the late nineteenth century, towards creating garden cities. The most outstanding among many enlightened practitioners was Ebenezer Howard. He proposed the creation of garden cities which became the forerunners of those suburban communities which have developed around London. Later, similar minded movements introduced this idea to the United States where a number of such garden city communities were developed. Naturally, these American communities were modified versions of the original British models, reflecting the availability of land as well as the beginning of an automobile-determined society. In essence, they were the forerunners of what we now know as the American suburbs.

Recently there has been a growing inquiry into the new American phenomenon referred to as "Edge-Cities" wherein new suburban communities, having sprung fully grown on the edge of larger cities, are born fully empowered politically, capable as well as willing to contest the supremacy of the nearby large city. In all cases, suburbs and "Edge-Cities" are attempts at finding urban solutions that will be spiritually, as well as economically, fulfilling. To date we have evidence that none of the models built so far has satisfactorily succeeded. Moreover, we have great evidence that many of the new cities created from zero to become capitals, such as Brasilia and Ahmedabad, have been resounding failures. It is only man's infinite capacity for adaptation that lets them limpingly survive.

Therefore, there is a need to develop new models. Today's electronic means make it possible for a very large number of professions to perform their tasks from home, or from satellite offices, without the need of direct presence at headquarters. By the same token, it is no longer necessary for headquarters

141

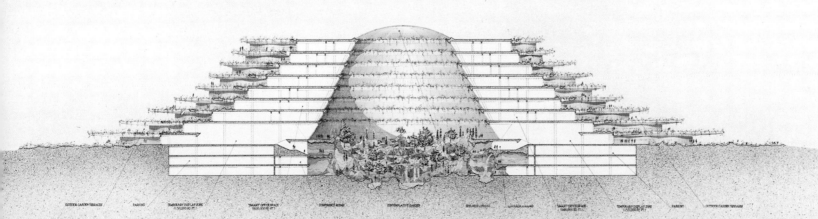

OUTDOOR GARDEN TERRACES   PARKING   TEMPORARY DISPLAY ZONE (1,50,000 SQ FT)   SMART OFFICE SPACE   CONFERENCE ARENA   CONTEMPLATIVE GARDEN   SHELTERED PLAZA   LANDSCAPE ISLAND   SMART OFFICE SPACE   TEMPORARY DISPLAY ZONE (1,50,000 SQ FT)   PARKING   OUTDOOR GARDEN TERRACES

0   20

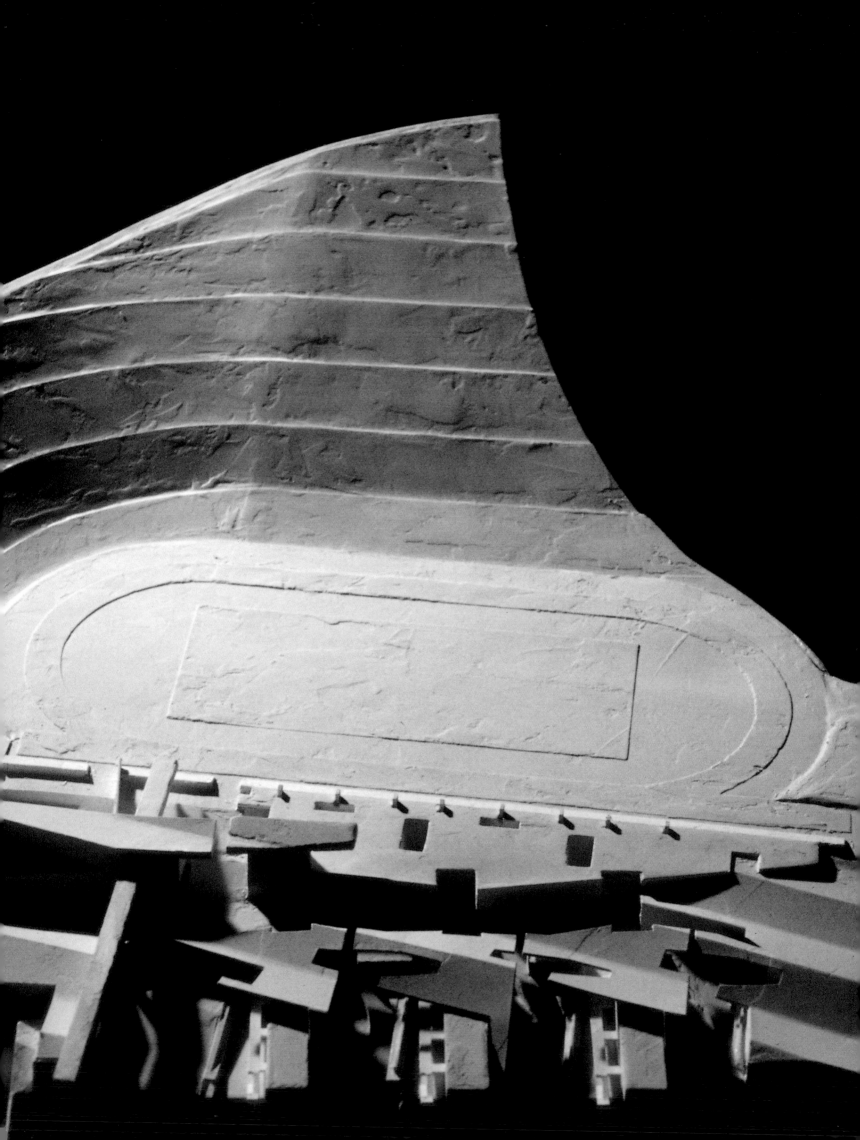

MORPHOSIS

Los Angeles, California, USA

Founded in 1974 by Thom Mayne and Michael Rotondi, and now run by Thom Mayne alone, Morphosis belongs to an Angelino architectural tradition which seeks to create new relationships between man and nature in a given urban context. Its work is rooted in forms where deconstructionist allusions can be found alongside a strong sense of drama. This aesthetic is exemplified in Kate Mantilini's Restaurant and the underground extension to the Cedars Sinai Hospital.

Diamond Ranch High School, Pomona, California

Diamond Ranch High School focuses on the desire to take advantage of the natural beauty of the site by integrating the playing fields and the buildings with the surrounding hillsides. The aim is to create a dynamic built environment to foster maximum social interaction between students, teachers, administration and the community. It should also provide a flexible teaching environment.

The intention was to create a building that would be perceived as "at one with the site" rather than "on top of the site." By reshaping the topography with outdoor playing fields, public spaces and a continuous undulating surface, Morphosis attempted to create a cohesive ensemble of building and landscape. In a similar manner, the building is integrated with its users through the courtyards and a pedestrian street which encourages interaction while fostering flexibility within the learning community. The project is also presented as a tangible way of preserving nature.

Opposite
Diamond Ranch High School
Pomona, California, USA.
View of the model.

Computer perspective.

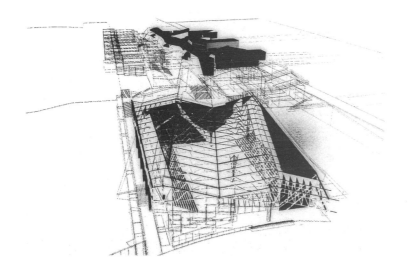

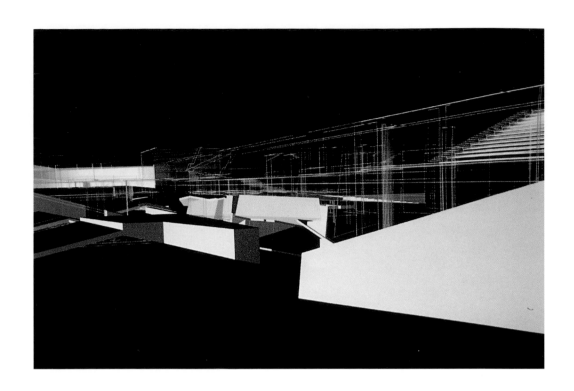

Diamond Ranch High School
Pomona, California, USA.
Perspectives.

Opposite
Aerial view of the model.

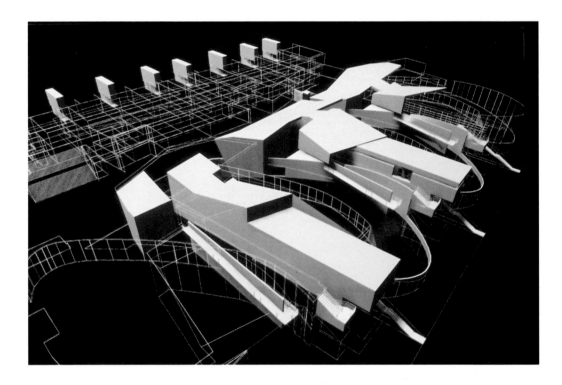

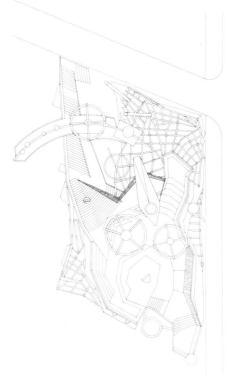

MASAHARU TAKASAKI

Tokyo, Japan

Masaharu Takasaki's response to the visual and structural chaos of Japanese cities is to invoke the power of nature, but without approaching anything like the ideas of the "organic" that are entertained in the west. His buildings are highly complex structures, executed in moulded metal and glass, with the occasional prominent timber element, which invites their colonisation by nature. He believes in architecture as a social art, "a form through which people are incited to realise their own visions of cosmos, nature and themselves."

Earth Architecture, Tokyo, Japan

For the Earth Architecture project, extensive psychological studies were undertaken. The architectural spaces created are the result of detailed consideration of how to combine and arrange "open domains" and "closed domains", meetings and partings, so as to facilitate and to keep a balance between the symbiosis and independence of individuals that will induce favourable personal relations and improve the quality of the activities performed there.

The site commands Mt. Fuji far to the west. The view of the mountain – the spiritual symbol of eternity – is incorporated into the architecture so that it can be shared by the residents and the neighbouring community; this also renforces awareness of the need for a symbiosis between them.

Earth Architecture is like a mountain, with its ground surface and its vegetation. The "Sky Plaza" is open to the community and embodies residents' willingness to share community spaces. There are no units with conventional floor plans: only free spaces with core facilities are proposed.

Earth Architecture
Tokyo, Japan.

Opposite
Above
Aerial view of the complex.
Below
Upper level circulation paths.
Left
Site plan.

Opposite
South elevation.

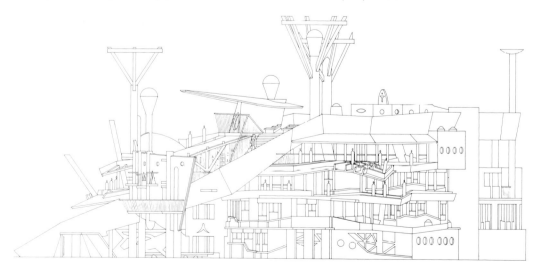

SIR RICHARD ROGERS

London, Great Britain
Tokyo, Japan

Since the revelation of the Pompidou Centre which he designed with Renzo Piano, Sir Richard Rogers' career has led him to construct major projects throughout Europe, the United States and Japan. He is the most flamboyant of all the so-called "high-tech" architects, as the Lloyd's Building in London, one of his masterpieces, testifies. But throughout his work, he has also consistently addressed underlying issues of urban planning. Over the last few years, Rogers has been particularly preoccupied with the question of how to control light and internal climate in his buildings, constantly on the look out for solutions that might be derived from the latest progress in automated information systems and new building materials.

The Architecture of the Future
Essay

I am searching for an architecture which will express and celebrate the ever-quickening speed of social, technical, political and economic change; an architecture of permanence and transformation where urban vitality and economic dynamics can take place, reflecting the changing and overlapping of functions; building as a form of controlled randomness which can respond to complex situations and relationships. Such architecture can be partially achieved by the zoning of buildings into long-life served and short-life servant activities.

The creation of an architecture which incorporates the new technologies entails breaking away from the platonic idea of a static world, expressed by the perfect finite object to which nothing can be added or taken away, a concept which has dominated architecture since its beginning. Instead of Schelling's description of architecture as frozen music, we are looking for an architecture more like some modern music, jazz or poetry, where improvisation plays a part, an indeterminate architecture containing both permanence and transformation.

The best buildings of the future, for example, will interact dynamically with the climate in order better to meet the users' needs and make optimum use of energy. More like robots than temples, these apparitions with their chameleon-like surfaces insist that we rethink yet again the art of building. Architecture will no longer be a question of mass and volume but of lightweight structures whose superimposed transparent layers will create form so that constructions will be effectively dematerialised.

To date – and here I include early Modernism – architectural concepts have been founded on linear, static, hierarchical and mechanical order. Today we know that design based on linear reasoning must be superseded by an open-ended

153

architecture of overlapping systems. This systems approach allows us to appreciate the world as an indivisible whole. We are, in architecture as in other fields, approaching a holistic ecological view of the globe and how we live on it.

In architecture, invisible micro-electronics and bio-technology are replacing industrial mechanical systems. We shall soon be living in a world so non-mechanical that buildings such as Lloyds of London, which is generally considered too innovative, will seem outdated and look old-fashioned.

Buildings, the city and its citizens will be one inseparable organism sheltered by a perfectly fitting, ever-changing framework. Posts, beams, panels and other structural elements will be replaced by a seamless continuity. These mobile, changing robots will possess many of the characteristics of living systems, interacting and self-regulating, constantly adjusting through electronic and bio-technological self-programming.

Present day concern for single objects will be replaced by concern for relationships. Shelters will no longer be static objects, but dynamic frameworks. Accommodation will be responsive, ever-changing and ever-adjusting. Cities of the future will no longer be zoned as today in isolated single-activity ghettos; rather, they will resemble the more richly layered cities of the past. Living, work, shopping, learning and leisure will overlap and be housed in continuous, varied and changing structures.

In the case of architectural structures, responsive systems, acting much like muscles flexing in a body, will reduce mass to a minimum by sifting loads and forces with the aid of an electronic nervous system which will sense environmental changes and register individual needs.

Today, automatic pilots in aeroplanes can monitor all control functions and environmental parameters many times a second, continuously adapting and modifying the aircraft control systems to achieve optimal flight and passenger comfort. The future is here, but its impact on architecture is only just beginning to be felt.

Michael Davies, one of my partners, has described the experience of living in a responsive building of the future:

> "Look up at a spectrum-washed envelope, whose surface is a map of its instantaneous performance, stealing energy from the air with an irridescent shrug, rippling its photogrids as a cloud runs across the sun, a wall which, as the night chill falls, fluffs up its feathers and, turning white on its north face and blue on the south, closes its eyes but not without remembering to pump a little glow down to the night porter, clear a view patch for the lovers on the south side of level 22 and so turn 12 per cent silver just before dawn."

It is not popular to link the economy and consumption with culture, and to suggest that today it is the accounting system that dictates to the Arts. Yet I firmly believe that to achieve a new cultural enlightenment, one which includes architecture, it will be necessary to redefine the balance between capital, labour, the planet and its poor.

I confess my opposition to our present exploitative economic system and my faith and unshaken conviction that a global community in which art and science are harnessed to serve the common good would represent the most beautiful and enlightening achievement of the human spirit.

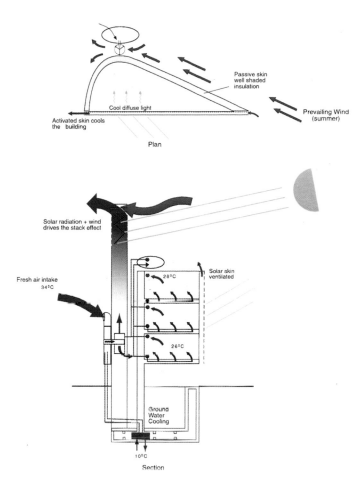

Passive skin
well shaded
insulation

Cool diffuse light

Prevailing Wind
(summer)

Activated skin cools
the building

Plan

Solar radiation + wind
drives the stack effect

Fresh air intake
34°C

28°C

Solar skin
ventilated

26°C

Ground
Water
Cooling

10°C

Section

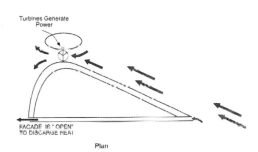

Turbines Generate
Power

FACADE IS "OPEN"
TO DISCARGE HEAT

Plan

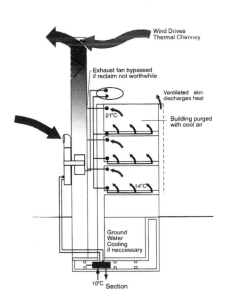

Wind Drives
Thermal Chimney

Exhaust fan bypassed
if reclaim not worthwhile

Ventilated skin
discharges heat

21°C

Building purged
with cool air

14°C

Ground
Water
Cooling
if neccessary

10°C Section

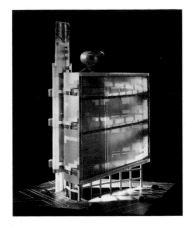

Turbine Tower
Tokyo, Japan
View of the model.

Left
Above
Plan and section
Operation on a summer day
Hot air is pre-cooled by the ground water
using a heat exchange system. Its
temperature is further reduced as it enters
the rooms by the chilled concrete slabs.
Used air is drawn out with the assistance
of sun and wind. As it passes through the
heat exchange system it reduces the
temperature and humidity of the air being
drawn in. The double skin cavity of the
southern facade traps the solar gain and
discharges it by way of ventilation top and
bottom

Below
Plan and section
Operation on a summer night
The concrete structure of the building is
chilled by flushing cool night air through it.
In mid-summer, the night air rises to a
temperature of 20°C and needs to be
chilled by the cool ground water. When
necessary, off peak electricity is used to
control the temperature of the water in the
basement tank which will rise slightly
during peak summer. The turbines are used
to generate energy.

Turbine Tower, Tokyo, Japan

The brief for the Turbine Tower, Tokyo, was for a dynamic landmark building that would stand out above the surrounding urban sprawl. The climate is extreme, cold in winter and hot and uncomfortably humid in summer. The main circular road for Tokyo passes along the southern side of the site.

The building aims to blend simple principles with new technology to achieve a responsive architecture that is both brilliant and optimistic, and makes the most of the environment and our capacity to harness it. Wind tunnel simulation was used to study how to accelerate the wind as it passed through the core so it could be used to drive turbines and power the building. Computer predictions have helped to create a fluid and dynamic architecture that is, in addition, self-sufficient.

Inland Revenue Offices, Nottingham, Great Britain

The Inland Revenue's new offices in Nottingham is a low energy building and is designed to be naturally ventilated; exposed concrete is used to moderate internal temperatures and water is used to cool down even further during hot summers. Fountains provide a cool background noise within the open atrium. Energy consumption is less than thirty per cent that of a conventional building.

Masterplan for Parc Bit, Majorca, Spain

The Masterplan for Parc Bit creates three small sustainable communities. A balanced cycle of activities is maintained over the day, as well as throughout the week, to create a 24-hour urban community and permanent public activity throughout the year.

Opposite
Inland Revenue Offices, Nottingham
Great Britain.
Two views of the model.

Below
Section.

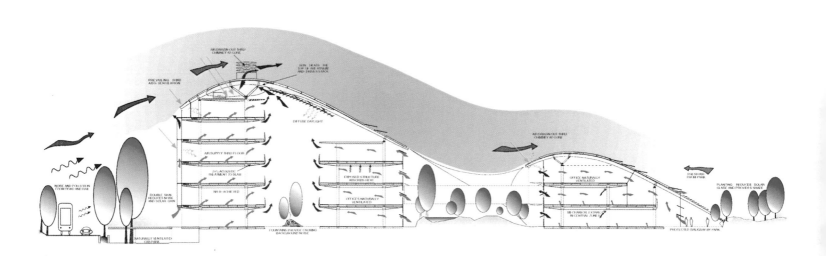

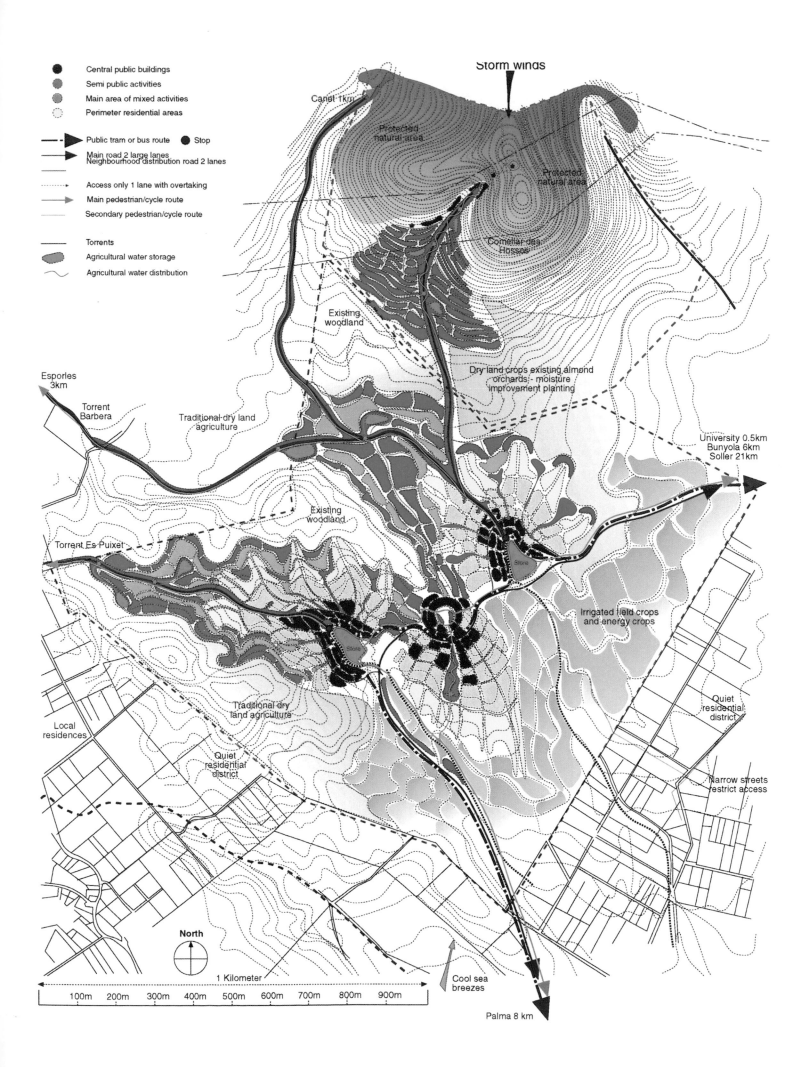

Storm winds

Central public buildings
Semi public activities
Main area of mixed activities
Perimeter residential areas

Public tram or bus route   Stop
Main road 2 large lanes
Neighbourhood distribution road 2 lanes

Access only 1 lane with overtaking
Main pedestrian/cycle route
Secondary pedestrian/cycle route

Torrents
Agricultural water storage
Agricultural water distribution

Canet 1km

Protected natural area

Protected natural area

Comellar des Hosses

Existing woodland

Esporles 3km

Torrent Barbera

Traditional dry land agriculture

Dry land crops existing almond orchards - moisture improvement planting

University 0.5km
Bunyola 6km
Soller 21km

Existing woodland

Torrent Es Puixet

Store

Store

Irrigated field crops and energy crops

Traditional dry land agriculture

Quiet residential district

Local residences

Quiet residential district

Quiet residential district

Narrow streets restrict access

North

1 Kilometer

100m 200m 300m 400m 500m 600m 700m 800m 900m

Cool sea breezes

Palma 8 km

Masterplan for Parc Bit
Majorca, Spain.

Opposite
The urban matrix is assembled by
superimposing different elements. The aim
is to integrate the elements with each
other so that the systems for water,
agriculture, movement, social mix and the
strategy for energy work well together.
The size of each village is defined by the
limits of easy walking distance from the
centre to the furthest point. The mix of
uses and social activities is gradually
diffused from a vibrant publicly focused
centre to the more peaceful, residential
areas. Renewable sources of energy are
used to generate power locally.

Above
Model of an individual unit.
Below
Urban matrix.

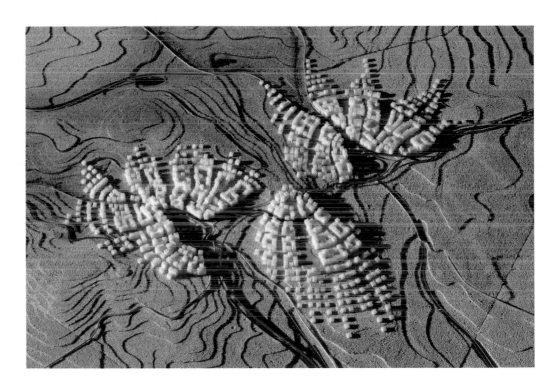

ITSUKO HASEGAWA

Tokyo, Japan

After working with the Japanese architects Kiyonori Kikutake* (the central figure of the Japanese Metabolism movement) and Kazuo Shinohara, Itsuko Hasegawa has developed her own highly original work. Her vocabulary is masterful and "absolutely modern": complex, lightweight structures, sophisticated superimposition of perforated metal sheets to produce shimmering effects, translucent glass imitating paper partition walls, and a virtuosic use of lighting effects based on spectral decomposition. Itsuko Hasegawa is one of the most original figures in contemporary architecture. Her work poses in new (specifically Japanese?) terms the unresolved question of the relationship between nature and civilization.

Opening up Architecture through Communication
A feminine approach
Essay

As if to compensate for the massive destruction of nature and cities, the extremely consumer-oriented Japanese society has become increasingly dependent on the mass media to simulate a new artificial environment. Simulation with its dream like imagery gives us the illusion of communicating with a self-fulfilling imagination. We continue to live in a fictional world, conscious that we can only have access to the beauty of nature through these media.

As this contrast becomes more and more obvious, people have started to ask questions: may not the simulated images themselves be in fact the cause of the deterioration of our quality of life? We have become aware of destruction on a global scale and have noticed that the nature that surrounds us does no longer sends out harmonious messages. Yet all man-made objects are ultimately derived from nature. Nature embraces every aspect of human existence. Man-made space merely provides different levels of environment and quality of life within nature. The state of that space is a reflection of the state of society.

Nowadays technical and scientific progress is too rapid for us even to notice the changes that take place. Whereas in the past we could evolve slowly in harmony with nature, the speed of present progress has accelerated the rate of its destruction. Architecture, on the other hand, from the eighteenth century to today, has aimed to homogenize the world, to make it transparent, and to deny gravity by achieving lightness of structure. How can architecture reorient itself as a life-supporting environment when we are all aware that we are living at the extremity of life? How can our imagination,

Opposite
Fruit Museum
Yamanashi, Japan.

S.T.M Building
Tokyo, Japan.

shaped by the new technological society, influence the outcome of architectural development?

Nothing will come out of that mysticism that is based on the seductions of technological progress, such as virtual reality. When we think about the world as a long-term continuum, an environment which should last forever, we realize how poor it has become today. Technological progress may eventually help to reveal inherent human potential and sensitivity. It may help to transform unconsciousness into consciousness. But today the difference between the human body and the world of simulation is increasing. As technology develops, this situation may lead to the isolation of human beings from their environment.

In order to break out of this dilemma, it is necessary to harness both physical human vigour and the multiplicity of media-created information environments. In architecture, this means giving equal importance to both "hardware" and "software".

Through experience, I have come to understand that many people willingly recognize the importance of their own environment, express concern about the state of public facilities that affect their daily lives, and want to participate to regain control over them. It is not sufficient for architects and city planners to implement their own personal beliefs. I am trying to introduce a new flexible architectural system which will be receptive to the diversity of individuals.

In the case of public buildings, the design normally follows the parameters outlined in an official programme. This kind of programme tends to be abstract and does not address the real needs of individual users. The resulting architectural design may be either mundane or monumental; in any case, it will not be responsive to reality. Like the city itself, public buildings must be able to accommodate the complexity and diversity of individual needs in order to attract people. In the past, public building projects were often used as an expression of the architect's ego, and their (lack of) social significance was hidden behind their supposed artistic values. In one sense, this approach can help to control the chaotic and unruly state of Japanese cities. But blind dependence on this approach can create an enormous rift between owners and users.

The current confusion of the Japanese urban environment is the result of the post-war interpretation of democracy, of a selfish possessiveness by individuals and corporations, and of the lack of communal consensus. The reason why large civil engineering, new-town and urban redevelopment projects, carried out by governments during periods of high economic stability and growth have been so uninspiring and of such low design quality, can be traced back to the political reality of Japan. A hierarchical decision-making process excludes anything that does not neatly fit the prototypes of national uniformity. Thus we encounter, everywhere in this country, what my English friend Peter Cook calls "garbage" urban landscapes.

Although the central government promoted the idea of urban diversity in the 1980s, it was only a modified centralism; and as the subservience of local communities to the central government became more concrete, the sense of local powerlessness grew stronger. However, some communities have embarked upon their own development plans in an entrepreneurial spirit. In those communities, the citizens cooperate with the authorities, and are critical of them too. We feel that this kind of communication could be used as a tool to alter drastically the way in which social architecture is planned. Both architects and individual citizens can experiment with mechanisms for assembling various materials and realize together a shared vision through the mutual experience of discord. Strategically speaking, we must create a process for returning public buildings to their users, involving them in decision-making and making them recognize their active involvement in the building process.

There are some architects who claim that architectural integrity bears no relationship to practicality and that architecture can be beautiful independently of any human involvement. Such narcissistic attitudes can only diminish the quality of architecture. They fully deserve the oft-heard criticism that architects do not have a social conscience.

One factor that led to the successful establishment of communication on the Shonandai Cultural Centre project was that we all shared a common sense of "architecture as second nature", which we used as the guiding principle for our design. Our cities are different from physically static European cities. Ours is an abstract form of nature, and their architecture retains a flexible relationship with natural phenomena such as the wind, water and topography. Architecture is a vessel for people's rich and ambiguous emotional responses, as well as for the changing seasons, climate, and the mysteries of the universe. We might call it a poetic machine.

In fact, I am more interested in creating a common dream through architecture than in regaining social acceptance for my profession. It is clear to me that my attitude towards architecture is not that of an exclusive dogma but consistently ad hoc, so that it is inclusive of many conflicting notions at the same time. My architectural reality is based on popular rationalism with a multipolar value system and is not the orthodox nationalism of a single value system. This attitude requires a change of architectural paradigm if we are to understand the unorganized forces of consciousness and embody the diversity of every group so that it can function as a constructive force.

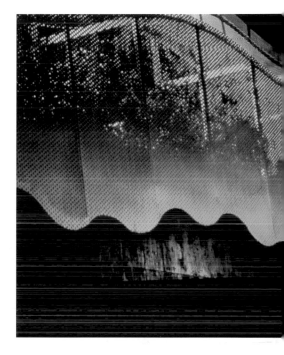

Fruit Museum, Yamanashi, Japan

Three structures with differing characteristics are aligned on a shallow south east slope offering a wonderful view of Mount Fuji. They are a tropical greenhouse, an atrium event space, and an educational workshop for teaching. The greenhouse is a shelter in the shape of a deformed globe, while the atrium is a saucer-shaped glass shelter with loose curves. The workshop is a transparent rectilinear building encased in a lopsided, egg-shaped pergola over which fruit-bearing lianas crawl freely.

House at Higashitamagawa
Japan.

Exhibition Pavilion, Nagoya, Japan

Designed as a temporary structure that was to be demolished after four months, the Nagoya Exhibition Pavilion comprises a theatre with 270 seats and a hanging garden. The site appeared shrouded in a light mist, changing as one approached into a garden enveloped in clouds and trees.

The architect's objective was to create a space that would allow a sort of coexistence with nature by using lightweight, translucent materials and "membranes" that allow the light, wind and sound to penetrate through them into the space inside. The visitor could thus "experience all those emotions that rationalism has forgotten, the sense of well-being offered by nature and by the sublime music of the universe".

Exhibition Pavilion
Nagoya, Japan.

Shonandai Cultural Centre, Fujisawa, Japan

For the Shonandai Cultural Centre, Itsuko Hasegawa has tried to produce a concentration of latent allusions to nature, which function like human memories. These allusions have been recreated through a project for "architecture as latent nature", in the form of an artificial hill (architecture as topography). "Rethinking architecture means recreating it according to a new natural order, so that it is richer than the topography it replaces, and is also a memorial to the segment of nature that has been destroyed. The building expresses itself as a means Hot communication with nature, as a means also to pay homage to the continuity of life on its most primitive level. In practice, I tried to imagine architecture as a second nature, which could react both to contemporary technology and to the spirit of the age".

Exhibition pavilion
Nagoya, Japan.

Shonandai Cultural Centre
Fujisawa, Japan.

Above
Night view of the interior.
Below
View of the piazza from the north tower.

Opposite
Above
The piazza by day, general view.
Below
"Metal vegetation".

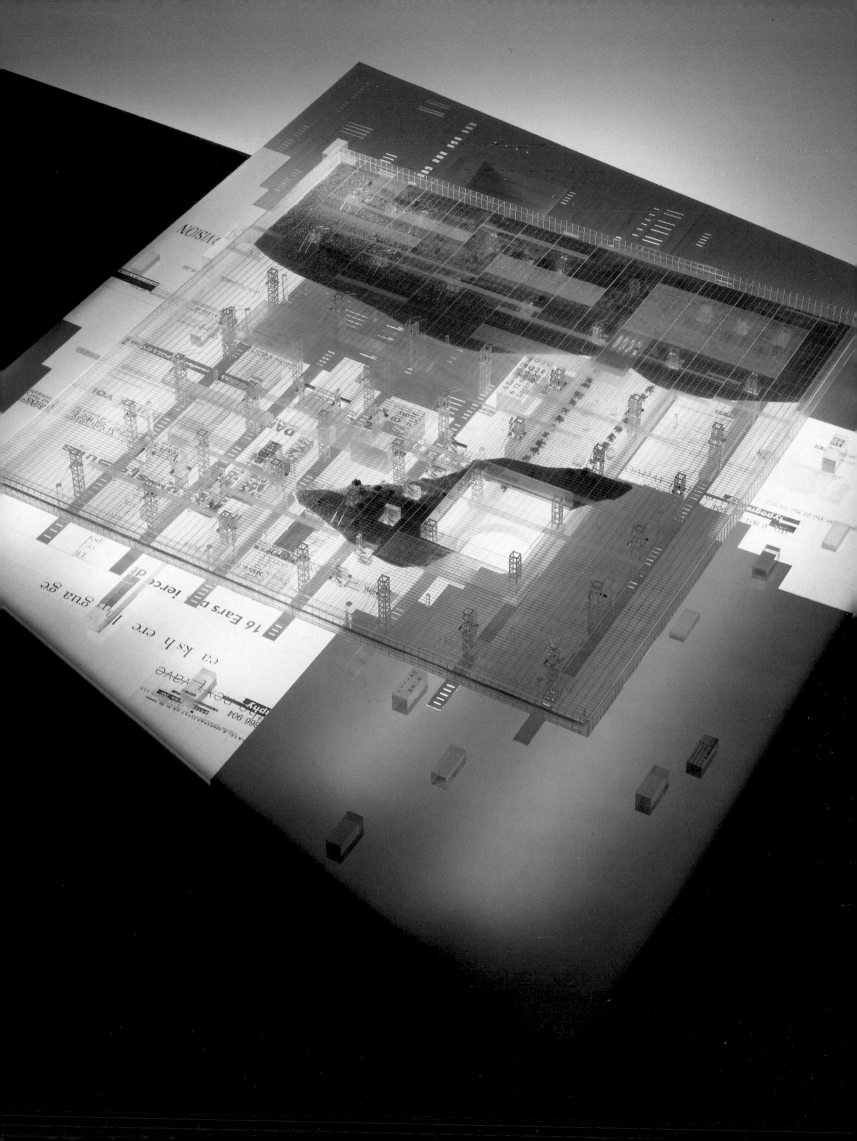

5. TOWARDS A PIXEL ARCHITECTURE

"C : \"
Bill Gates

Electricity and its scintillating effects had already given today's architects those brilliant and evocative tools of which Las Vegas and Shinjuku, Tokyo are the accepted icons. The development of the new media, the information networks (which boast their own architecture), the cathode tube and the profusion of images from every source (from micro to macrocosm) hold a double fascination for a whole generation of architects:

– the impact of the unique plasticity they create, revealing as yet unexplored possibilities for architecture;

– their less tangible impact on form (or rather the absence of form) which haunts the imagination, creating a ghostly aesthetic of disappearance.

Will architects know how to rise to the challenge of creating immaterial space? ∎

Opposite
Crystal Monolith
Yokohama, Japan.
Shin Takamatsu
View of the model.

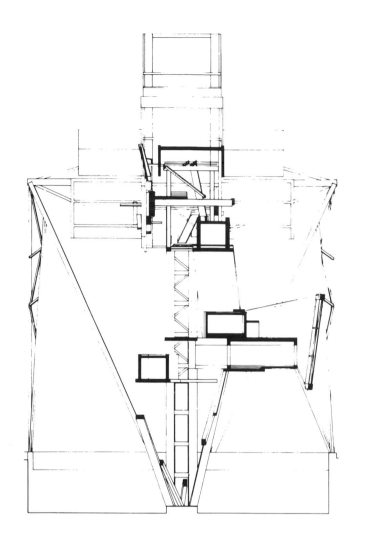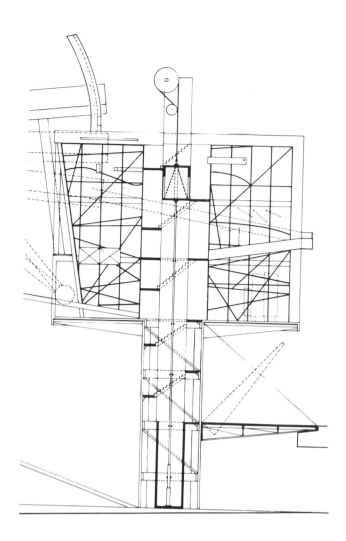

ASYMPTOTE ARCHITECTURE

New York, USA

Founded in 1987 in New York by Lise-Anne Couture and Hari Rashid, Asymptote Architecture set out to question the very basis of architecture, its methods and its goals, in a world whose traditional structures have been overturned by the information revolution. Asymptote projects, whatever form they take – systems (known as "optigraphs"), installations, or more traditional models and drawings – force us to confront modes of perception that have been modified by technology (and which are haunted by an obsession with surveillance). In their submissions to competitions for the Alexandria Library, the Moscow Theatre, the Groningen Court House, or the Spreebogen district of Berlin, Lise-Anne Couture and Hari Rashid address problems that are crucial for the future of architecture: the adequation of the traditional order of preoccupations with the environment, behaviour, functionality and even perfection, faced with the influence of new technologies. "Today, architectural forms emerge from a space of flux and fluidity".

Steel Cloud, Los Angeles, Californie, USA

The Steel Cloud or Los Angeles West Coast Gateway is typical of Los Angeles, a place construted of grand fictions and utopian fantasies. Inspired by optical machinery, flight simulation, and the technologies of surveillance, this episodic architecture seeks to reconfigure information, speed and the instantaneous into a new city-space. Here an anticipatory monument reveals an invisible site directly above the Hollywood Freeway as a place where "the super-rapid position of rest" of a closing millennium can be felt. This space for the post-information age, made up of infinitely oscillating fields devoid of perspective or depth, forms an architecture of ambiguity and anonymity amidst the noise and distraction of Los Angeles.

The Steel Cloud is not a monument to some militaristic conquest or political authority, rather it is a device to be filled and conquered by the human spirit, a living monument, accommodating galleries, libraries, theatres, cinemas, parks and plazas, each intersected by the fluid and transient city. Here aquariums and suspended landscapes oscillate to the arcane rhythms of the freeway. The Cloud itself, held together by cables, steel girders, harnesses and weights, counters the precarious shifting plates beneath it. This strange and disparate architecture is constantly being unfinished and resituated.

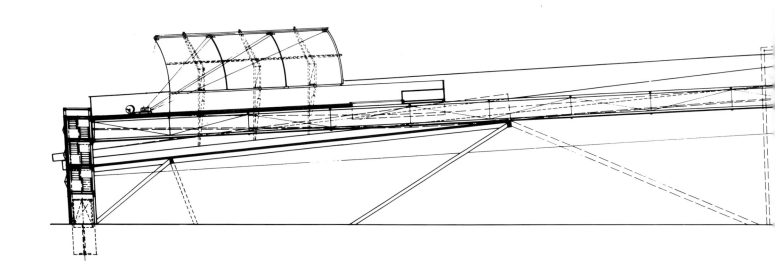

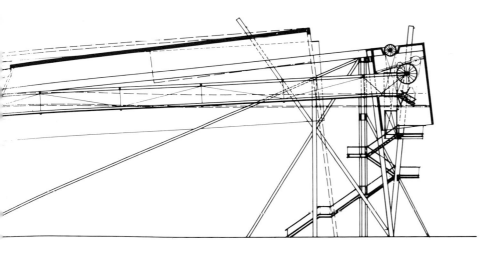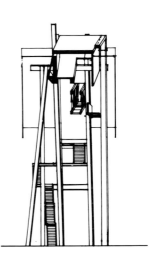

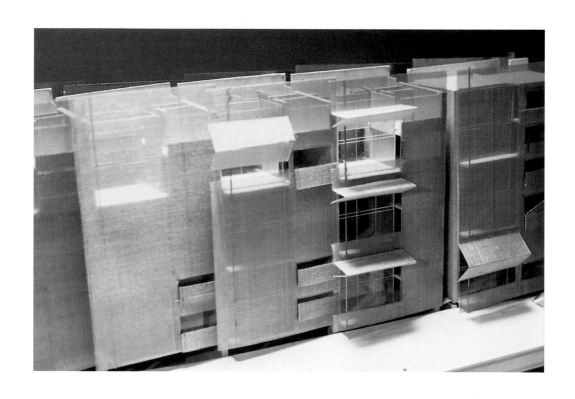

DILLER & SCOFIDIO

New York, USA

Elizabeth Diller and Paul Scofido trained in New York in the late seventies, in the poetic and polemical atmosphere of John Hedjuk's* Cooper Union. They have since developed their own very particular approach: their projects and installations are intended to decipher and interpret the rituals, institutions and discouse which maintain society in its current state of cohesion, but also to reveal the ideology underlying the events and assumptions that make up contemporary life.

The Gifu Housing Project, Gifu, Japan

Diller and Scofidio believe that the rhetoric of "variety" that accompanied the introduction of standardization in European Modernism was an illusion, which delivered anonymity instead. The economic constraints and inevitability of repetition, which come with standardization in social housing, however, need not lead to the erasure of the individual dwelling. Their Gifu Housing Project, Japan, articulates distinctly in plan, and positions uniquely in section, each of its one hundred units.

The "reptilian" building is made up of rectangular stacks that interlock leaving a discrepancy of 1.5 degrees which accumulates into a shallow curve. Each unit is offset from the next by one metre to leave space for the entry door, a surface always approached frontally, in keeping with tradition. The outermost skin of diaphanous overlapping "scales" of perforated metal is mobile to the south. To the North, it serves to privatize the ramping system along which each unit is placed at a unique elevation.

The Tower of Babel, New York, USA

The Tower of Babel addresses the question of the fate of cultural diversity in our progressively mono-cultural world. It is a permanent installation planned for the corner of 42nd Street and Eighth Avenue, comprising a stack of video screens which feature giant speaking mouths, each reciting a sequence of adages on the theme of language in the most prominent languages spoken in the United States. The conglomeration of voices will be audible as an indistinct blur, except for the voice closest to the street. After each adage is spoken, the images in the stack will drop one interval from the top. The tower inverts the proposition of the biblical Tower of Babel in which language is used as a weapon against the earliest mono-culture in order to secure the heavens from the common people. Rather, the project aestheticizes the very sound of babel and through the successive de-lamination of voices, the rich complexities of communication are emphasized.

175

Jump Cuts, San Jose, California, USA

Jump Cuts will be a permanent facade for the world's largest Cineplex theatre planned for San Jose, California, composed of sculptural, electronic and video components which will broadcast images and texts, both informative and contemplative, to the street. Using liquid crystal technology, the facade will intermittently exchange the view of the activity in the lobby seen from the street with video views of the street taken from within the building – thus turning the building inside-out like a glove, electronically. Film extracts, trailers and adverts will also be used.

The Tower of Babel
New York, USA.
Temporary installation.

Right
View of the model.

Opposite
Jump Cuts
San Jose, California, USA.
Video facades.

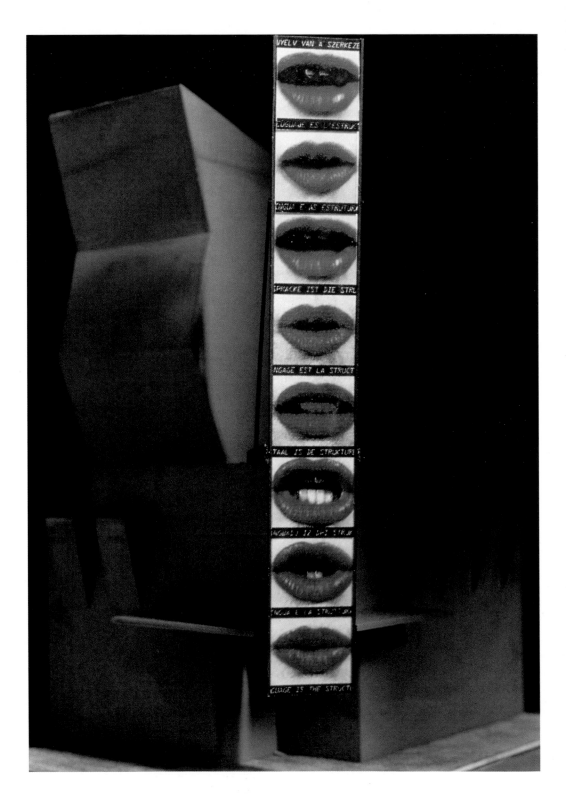

176

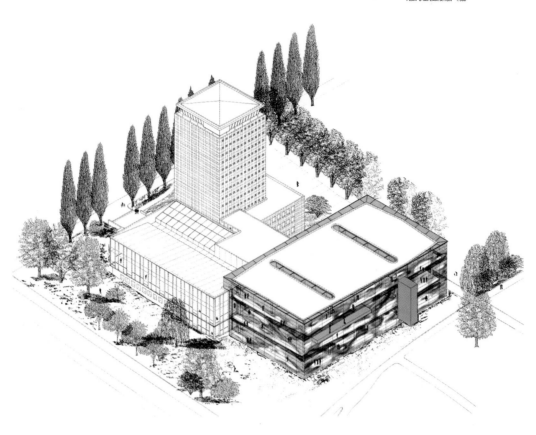

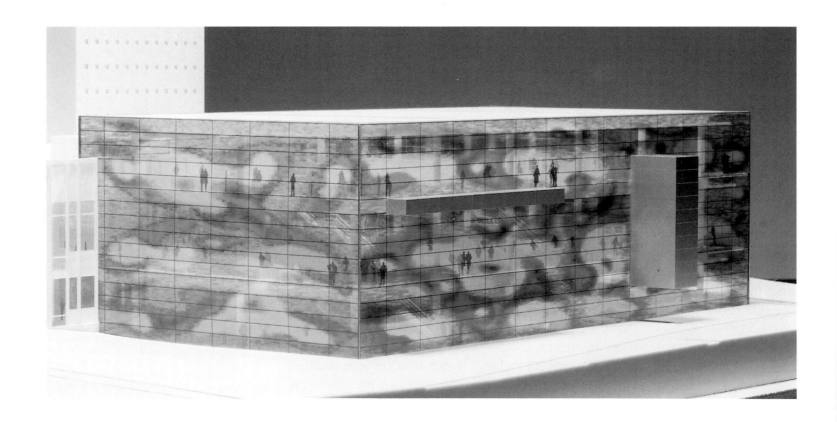

DU BESSET AND LYON

Paris, France

From their apprenticeship with their prestigious elders, Jean Nouvel and Frank Gehry, Pierre Du Besset and Dominique Lyon learned the discipline of an approach that explores all the possibilities of the programme and the site and a great liberty of form without loss of control. Since they established their own practice in 1984 they have worked on several modest but difficult projects (the restoration of the Rotonde des Vétérinaires in the Parc de La Villette, and the Le Monde newspaper building, both in Paris) and competition entries (the Jussieu libraries, the Dijon University Campus, etc.)

The Mediatheque in Orleans (1994) reveals their sound grasp of urban projects and their ability to transform a banal programme into a subtle building endowed with a moving fragility.

Extension to the University Library, Dijon, France

A library gathers information and organizes access to it. The pleasure it gives lies in the perception of this accumulation.

The extension to the University Library in Dijon places the user at the heart of this system. He can see all that is on offer at a glance and without being overwhelmed: on the facade he can see monochrome motifs that are free, mobile, translucid or transparent; the floors and the ceilings float within this fluid skin. The continuity of the coloured motifs is visible beneath the floors and the activities taking place on other levels can be guessed at.

Mediatheque, Orleans, France

A mediatheque is a place where people find for themselves the means by which to increase their knowledge. The Orleans Mediatheque seeks to clarify the idea of this process which cannot take place unless the user demonstrates his curiosity. Thus he must proceed in stages. The architectural process corresponds to the intellectual process: each functional space in the programme (lending room, reading room, periodicals room, cafeteria, etc.) is identified by very simple means: a symmetrical plan, a single colour. Each space is treated as a room. There are as many rooms as there are elements in the programme.

Each room has its raison d'être and at the same time integrates the presence of its immediate neighbours. They form a whole to which nothing can be added and from which nothing can be taken away, resulting in a simple form that binds them together. But the resulting form is not unequivocal. Culture cannot be grasped globally. The various rooms rebel, jut out and give the building a monumental dimension.

Extension to the University Library
Dijon, France.

Above
Facade in screenprinted glass
(distorted vision).

Opposite
Above
General axonometric.
Below
Model of the library.

179

Mediatheque, Orleans
France.

Above
The Mediatheque in context.
Below
Perforated metal sunshades to filter light
and vision.

Opposite
View over the cityscape from inside.

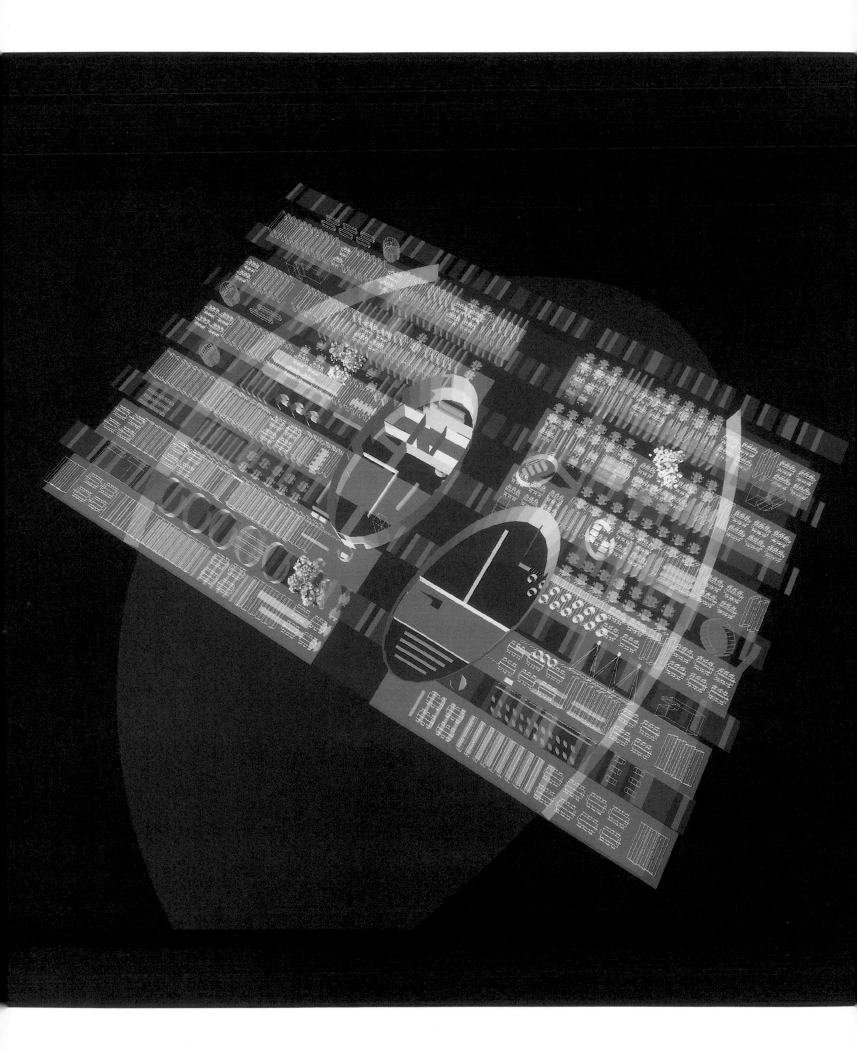

TOYO ITO

Tokyo, Japan

Since the 1970s, Toyo Ito has been exploring a number of questions that have never received a definitive answer: how to define an introverted domestic space (his U-shaped house), how to re-read modernity (how to *build* Le Corbusier's Domino House), etc. Today, he is working against a homogenized society in which life is entirely simulated and has thus lost its meaning. How can we create real architecture in a universe in which objects are losing their reality? How can we create a permanent space appropriate to a society in perpetual flux? Ito tries to answer these questions by emphasizing the ephemeral and the fictional. His idea of "nirvana" is situated at the furthest limits of technological control. The result is a fluctuating immaterial architecture, sensitive to the elements, and integrating modern methods of producing images and sounds.

Sendai Mediatheque, Japan

The Mediatheque at Sendai is a place where the primitive body and the virtual body reacting to electronic flux can be combined and organized. The design does not emphasize architectural form, but highlights the structure as a natural flux as well as an electronic matching.

The building consists of seven layers one on top of the other, each matching a different communication situation, using different media. There are twelve tubes controlling and organizing the layers. They are flexible structures, at the same time providing vertical circulation and flow space for all kinds of energy and information, light and sound. The building is surrounded by a skin that controls the interior environment.

The artist Laurie Anderson says: "The body of a modern human being consists of an electronic flux". Since ancient times, our body has been linked to nature as a fluid consisting of water and air. Now the body as electronic flux is changing the forms of communication, but our primitive body still seeks after beautiful light or a cool breeze.

Tower of the Winds, Yokohama, Japan

The Tower of the Winds in Yokohama is a remodelling of an existing tower built for ventilation and water storage twenty years ago. It is sheathed in perforated aluminium and the external walls are covered with acrylic mirror plates. More than two thousand electric light bulbs are controlled by computer to respond to the wind, noise, and temperature. During the day, the aluminium panels reflect light and accentuate the simple form of the cylindrical structure. As the lamps are lit at dusk, a kaleidoscopic effect is created. The aluminium panels become an almost transparent film and the tower loses its physical form and is changed into a virtual image. It has no specific architectural form and may be compared to visual background music.

Opposite
Two Libraries at Jussieu
Paris, France.
Computer axonometric.

Overleaf
Sendai Mediatheque
Japan.
Section revealing the structure.

Tower of the Winds
Yokohama, Japan.
Two night views.

JEAN NOUVEL

Paris, France

Jean Nouvel achieved recognition in the 1980s with a series of buildings each of which differed in their form and connotations. Nouvel sees himself as an architect of the specific: a specific programme and project conditions are matched by a specific response. This principled stance is accompanied by a clear-cut belief that architecture, rather than being an autonomous discipline, is permeated by, and ought to mirror, social realities.

Architects must try to take into account the free flow of images, miniaturisation, automation, speed, the conquest of space, and the emerging symptoms of a new popular culture (rap music, sport, etc.).

Nouvel's architecture emphasises material and light over the interplay of volume and space. It tends to dissolve the materiality of the world in a subtle combination of reflections, refractions, superimpositions, dilutions, flashing signs and moving colours.

Mutations
Essay

The concept of architecture is going through a process of massive change, barely discernible amidst the haze and dust clouds raised by the urban cataclysm that has struck our planet. Population explosion, industrial revolution and its direct consequences, urban encroachment of rural areas, the global market and global communication with their burgeoning networks: these are some of the reasons which explain why, in the 20th century, four or five times more buildings have been built than in the entire previous course of human history.

The transformation is profound, and the scope of architecture has been considerably extended. Today, the built fabric, which has grown up despite appalling conditions, is the visible consequence of an accelerated sedimentation. The facts stare us in the face: the inevitable has become reality. Once again, *topos* has taken precedence over *logos* . New building has been designed in difficult conditions, with barely a thought; the definitive criterion has been above all sheer urgency.

Much has been built, and in an utterly haphazard way. Conscientious architects have repeatedly criticised this state of affairs. But what have they proposed instead? Solutions which are either clinical, like Le Corbusier's Cité radieuse (Radiant City)*, ecological, like Frank Lloyd Wright's Broadacre City*, or plastic, like De Stijl's * colour and form chart.

In fact, since the 15th-century invention of the city as an architectural object, History has repeatedly demonstrated that the city lends itself less and less to an overall plan; that, on the contrary, it is the result of economic forces operating on a given territory, forces which brook no resistance, least of all that of aesthetic or humanist *a priori* theories. Besides, the tangible consequences of such theories are not always devoid of ambiguity.

Thus, in a roundabout, haphazard, expedient way, forms have emerged. These forms are often chaotic, yet still at times decipherable: it is even possible to attempt to link them to a secret order from which a fatal beauty occasionally wells up, often as the direct result of a given geographical context.

The new image of the world which has taken shape before our eyes is simultaneously fascinating, disturbing, occasionally disconcerting and sometimes even disgusting and repellent; yet it is difficult to deny it those qualities usually reserved for veritable "concretion-creations".

What is clear today, and inevitably concerns us as regards the future of our discipline, is that the *tabula* is no longer *rasa* . The early years of the century were swept along on the euphoric wave of industrial expansion and burgeoning modernity. Today we are no longer faced with inventing the city of tomorrow on the basis of aesthetic, cultural and ethical criteria that are shared by a generation for whom progress is a driving force with boundless possibilities. We have to face the fundamental truth that modern cities have been invented without us, at times, in spite of us. They are the outcome of evolution, a new layer on the planet's crust, perhaps signifying the dawn of a new era – the urban age.

The architectural vision of the city is in need of radical rethinking. It is high time to admit that, in the present historical conjuncture, a typological and morphological approach to cities merely leads to archaism, to the building of pre-urban-age cities. It can no longer serve as a serious conceptual basis. More than ever, it is the architect's duty to be aware of life, to form an opinion as to its direction and evolution. And for the architect, for whom 'doing' is as important as 'knowing', who has to translate a project into brick and mortar, and who is confronted with the contradiction between the rapidly evolving city and the lethargic pace of the architectural process itself, this is a complex and extremely awkward problem. The founding texts by Alberti[*] and More[*] still have a certain mystique for us: the former grounded architecture as an autonomous discipline, the latter as a prophetic, humanist, libertarian vision. How can an increasingly wide and fragmented knowledge be reconciled with a more and more pervasive praxis? No one is expected to achieve the impossible. The architect cannot simultaneously be philosopher, scientist, and artist; nor perform the role of one-man-band – planner, designer, engineer, economist, lawyer, site manager – that architectural practice implies. Yet Alberti's gamble of renouncing a global vision in favour of a restricted, autonomous, purely professional approach has had to yield to historical fact. Alberti's doctrine held sway for half a millenium. How is the architect to respond today?

Any contemporary definition of architecture would have to start by stating what architecture does not involve. Emergent modern architecture sought to create a new world; overreaching its capacities, it failed in this ambition, unable to grasp that the world does not belong to the architect but that, on the contrary, the architect belongs to the world. Architecture is a modification and an extension of the world, a victory over chaos, an involuntary adventure. Each era has to reinvent its own means of evolution and harness related knowledge. To succeed in such an adventure, one must draw upon all the resources for knowledge of contemporary thought.

Conference Centre
Tours, France.

Obviously, for the architect, who is necessarily grounded in reality, science is useful in its everyday applications. Technological and technical progress, and the introduction of new materials with revolutionary properties represent, if it may be put this way, grounds for calling what he knows into question. In its relationships with pure and applied science, architecture tends towards a performative synergy.

At this stage, a new factor intervenes in the evolution of our discipline, a factor rarely taken into consideration on a historical or critical level: although architecture has taken on board this performative synergy, it no longer stands in awe of modernity. The fascination which technical prowess, revered as a symbol, inspired in the pioneering modern architects has had its day. Nowadays, although the role of the engineer has lost none of its power, nobility, or prestige, the technical effort involved need no longer be revealed. Architecture is expected to be self-evident, to be guided by something other than sheer contingency or harsh constructional realities.

The very concept of the city has exploded. The city has become a cosmos, a galaxy of innumerable individual units, where things are in a perpetual flux of formation and disintegration. We have to invent its evolutionary processes, to assess change, to go along with this change or act against it. I sense today that the evolution of these galaxies is at a standstill and that, in the future, they will only develop through a process of iteration, alteration, or revelation. This implies an end to long-term planning, to standard blueprints, to zoning. It means that each urban decision will be the result of a binary choice between integration and differentiation.

The notions of integration and differentiation in turn imply a very special kind of commitment on the part of the architects called upon to choose between them. Only "conceptual" architects who as a matter of principle have conducted the most detailed analyses and imagined the widest range of possibilities will be capable of choosing with complete lucidity.

If we ponder the future of architecture, we must also pose the awkward question of the relationship between History and modernity. The very definition of modernity is of necessity subject to perpetual change. Today, I would readily propose as an initial definition of modernity that it is the best possible way of making the most of our memory – a permanently updated diagnosis.

A second definition might run as follows: modernity is knowing, then choosing the right course and the swiftest possible implementation to take us in the direction of our evolving knowledge, within a framework of analysis and diagnosis.

An attempt may be made to define the criteria of evolution, to discuss the paradigms of modernity.

One of the first things to be noted is that space and form play an ever-diminishing role and that, on the other hand, light and material are assuming increasing importance. Simplicity and complexity are further paradigms. As form and space have been simplified and smoothed out, only a new level of interpretation will enable us to say to what extent an object, which may appear simple, is in fact more complex than we may have ever actually conceived. Or consider the paradigms of density and lightness. Things will be increasingly condensed: here, one could point to the tendency to miniaturisation and heightened performance, or again, to mechanisation and passive systems.

This leads me to the notions of "support" and "contribution": in a building, we have to determine which are the fixed and which the mobile elements.

Euralille
Station triangle, Lille, France.
Façade with screenprints and holographs.

The current trend is towards an increasingly clear-cut dissociation: in other words, "supporting" features include everything intended to last, while "contributing" features cover all those that are subject to rapid change.

More than ever today, architecture is political. Architects are, in their own way, politicians. At the same time, this democratic dimension should be kept distinct from the cultural dimension.

We will only change through a process of giving. Film-maker Wim Wenders has said that the most important and most under-estimated word of all is "kindness". I believe this to be true, I believe in the value of giving, I believe that architects today should not only be level-headed, but big-hearted at the same time.

Endless Tower, la Défense, Paris, France

The aesthetic of a double disappearance: an endless tower.

The human mind is obsessed and fascinated by infinity, eternally raising metaphysical questions: where does it begin? where does it end?

The tower is a metaphysical object. It calls the idea of a limit into question.

The tower vanishes into the ground, and springs out of it. The conditions governing the construction of an extremely high building reside in this twin dynamic of burial and emergence.

The building disappears into the firmament. The materials employed – opaque granite, polished, perforated aluminium, and clear, reflective glass – invest it with an immaterial, unreal aspect. Soaring higher and higher, it slowly fades from sight. The successive use of different materials emphasises the natural, graduated effect.

Floor by floor, the building dematerialises until the simple transparent wall at its very tip melts into the background of the sky.

The Cartier Foundation, Paris

The ghost of a park. Transparent. Inclusive. Behind the tall, glazed enclosure that has replaced the former uninterrupted wall, the trees emerge, part of the twenty-five-foot high shell against which they gently brush.

Cartier Foundation
Paris, France.
Day view

Chateaubriand's cedar stands alone, framed by two screens that mark the entrance. Passing under the cedar, visitors discover the trees surrounding the exhibition hall, another twenty-five-foot glazed building, as they take in the full depth of the site.

In summer, the large sliding windows are opened, transforming the hall into an extension of the gardens.

The sky itself appears transparent. From the boulevard, the building seems like a shimmering halo against the backdrop of the sky, superimposed on which are real or virtual trees, as reflected and refracted by the glazed screens.

The architecture, with its finely woven glazing and steel, has an all-pervasive lightness, blurring the tangible limits of the building, eclipsing the impression of a solid volume in a poetically evanescent haze, and once again opening out the pleasant prospect of a fine garden long tucked away from sight. It is an architecture which deliberately adopts a clear stance in relation to the notion of transparency and its allegedly supine neutrality. When virtuality confronts reality, it is architecture's duty to courageously assume the image of contradiction.

Lyons Opera House, France

The modernisation of this 19th-century opera house, built in the very centre of town, provided the pretext for an architectural *tour de force*. The neo-classical facades were retained, preserving the building's integration with the surrounding urban fabric. The new theatre has tripled the original volume: part of the programme involved the provision of new spaces under the old building, while a semi-cylindrical luminous vault has been installed above. The cantilevered Italian auditorium and the public areas play on a register combining both familiar and novel sensations: the ritual dignity associated with the colours deployed – deep blacks, gold and red; the shimmering reflections of the suspended shell evoking the sleek refinement of a grand piano; the vertiginous escalators that run the full height of the building. The new Lyons opera house, with its striking silhouette, is intended to be a significant landmark in the urban centre and at the same time a refined and highly efficient working space.

Cartier Foundation
Paris, France.
Night view.

Cartier Foundation
Paris, France.

Above
The town seen from inside.
Below
Entrance to the building.

Opposite
Endless Tower
La Défense, Paris, France.
View of the model.

Page 196
Lyons Opera House,
France.

Above left
The building in the city.
Below left
The entrance hall.
Above right
The stalls.
Below right
Access areas.

Page 197
View of the building from the City Hall.

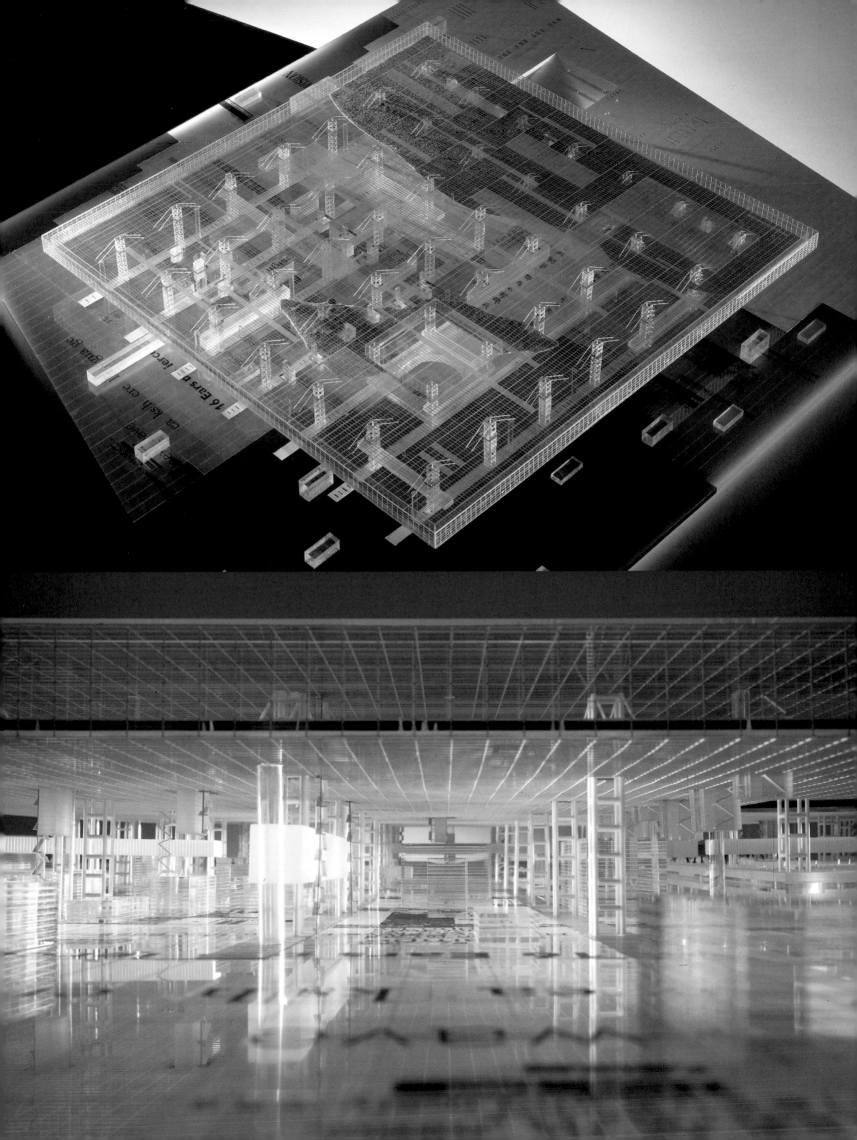

SHIN TAKAMATSU

Kyoto, Japan

Shin Takamatsu was educated in Kyoto, where he studied architecture, founding his own practice in 1980. He developed a highly personal style that was inspired by the heavy, massive and impressive machinery created by 19th-century engineering, as well as by mediaeval armour. His buildings were menacing forms, which evoked both Fritz Lang's film, *Metropolis*, and samurai masks. In them, he tried to offer a spatial summary of "the symptoms of what is wrong with the city".

More recently, influenced by "the volatile character of society and the consequent transformation of architecture", he has redirected his work towards the search for a "space of marginal activity", that is, a space that might escape from the strict confines of the programme. In the process, his work has grown lighter in material and in form, and acquired a new, almost evanescent geometrical simplicity.

Crystal Monolith, Yokohama, Japan

The Crystal Monolith is an architectural project which works to reinforce the collective memory. It is a design for an amusement park on an abandoned crude oil tank yard for the Yokohama Design Forum. The concept is to create an artificial sea in a 450 x 450 x 15 m (492 x 492 x 16 yds) glass box which floats 30 m (33 yds) above the ground.

A few decades from now, there may no longer be any unpolluted seas, and people may not even remember that there once was unpolluted sea.

Future Port City

Future Port City is a design for an airport and a Utopian city for the year 2050. The design meets the brief of satisfying the demand for the proper accommodation of new technologies, as extrapolated into the next millennium. The architect has tried to anticipate probable changes in the perception of space and time that may be generated by the revolution in speed.

Opposite
Crystal Monolith
Yokohama, Japan.

Above
Axonometric.
Below
Interior perspectives.

Overleaf
Future Port City

Left
Volume plan.
Right
View of the model.

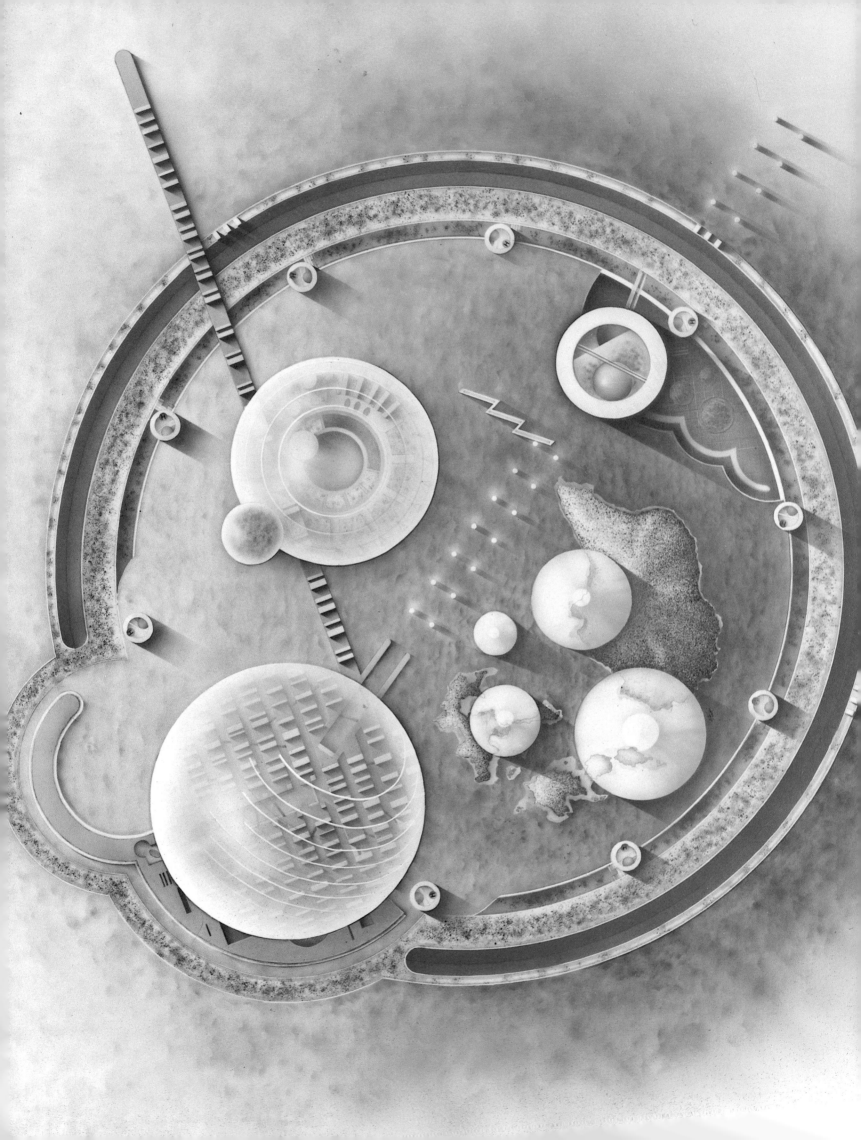

BIOGRAPHIES

ALSOP & STÖRMER

WILLIAM ALSOP

Born in 1947 in Northampton, Great Britain.
1969: Architectural Association Diploma, London.
1973-77: works with Cedric Price.
1979: creation of Alsop & Lyall.
1990: creation of Alsop & Störmer
Member of the Royal Institute of British Architects; fellow of the Royal Society of Arts; William Van Allen Medal for Architecture, New York.
Has taught at St-Martin's School of Art, at the Architectural Association, at Ball State University, Indiana, and at the University of Vienna.

JAN STÖRMER

Born in 1942 in Berlin, Germany.
1962: Diploma in Architecture and Engineering, Bremen, Germany.
1969: Founder member of Me-di-um Architecten, Hamburg.
1990: joins William Alsop.

Selected buildings and projects: Cardiff Bay Visitors' Centre, (1990); North Greenwich Museum, London; CrossRail Station, Paddington, London (1992).

EMILIO AMBASZ

Born in 1943 in Argentina.
1965: MA in architecture from Princeton University.
1970-76: Curator of Design at the Museum of Modern Art, New York. Exhibitions: *Italy: The New Domestic Landscape* (1972); *The Architecture of Luis Barragan* (1974), *The Taxi Project* (1976).
He has taught at Princeton University and at the Hochschule für Gestaltung, Ulm.
Selected buildings and projects: Mycal Sanda Cultural Centre, Japan; Museum of American Folk Art, New York; Conservatory, San Antonio Botanical Center, Texas (1988).

ARAKAWA AND MADELINE GINS

ARAKAWA

Born in 1936 in Japan.
1961: moves to New York.
1987: created Containers of Mind Foundation with Madeline Gins.
1994: inauguration of an «Arakawa» room at the Nordrhein-Westphalen Museum, Düsseldorf.
Chevalier of the Order of Arts and Letters (1986); John Simon Guggenheim Fellowship (1987-88); Belgian Critics' prize (1988).

MADELINE GINS

Born in 1941 in New York, USA.
1962: graduated Barnard College, New York.
1963: collaboration with Arakawa on the «Mechanism of Meaning» research project.
Has exhibited with Arakawa since 1972 in Europe, the USA and Japan.

Constructions: Ubiquitous Site "Nagi Ryoanji" Heart (Permanent Installation) Nagi MOCA, Japan (1994); Site of Reversible Destiny (theme park and house), Gifu, Japan (1995).

ASYMPTOTE ARCHITECTURE

LISE ANNE COUTURE

Born in 1959.
1986: M. Arch. from Yale University, USA.

1988-89: Muschenheim fellowship from the University of Michigan.
Has taught at the Frankfurt Städelschule, at the University of Michigan at Ann Arbor, at Barnard College,New York, at Harvard Graduate School of Design and at Parsons School of Design, New York.

HANI RASHID

Born in 1958.
1985: M.Arch from Cranbrook Academy of Art.
Has taught at the Royal Danish Academy of Copenhagen, at the Southern California Institute of Architecture at Los Angeles, at Harvard University and at Columbia University.
1987: creation of Asymptote Architecture in New York.

Selected projects and buildings: urban plan for city of Lanciano, Italy (1987); Steel Cloud, Los Angeles (winning competition entry, 1988); Alexandria Library, Egypt (competition entry 1989); Berlin Spreebogen, Germany (competition entry 1993).

PETER COOK

Born in 1936 at Southend-on-Sea, Great Britain.
1953-56: Bournemouth College of Art, Department of Architecture.
1960: Architectural Association Diploma, London.
1961: first *Archigram* magazine, followed by eight more published annually.
1962: joined Taylor Woodrow Design Group.
1968-76: Archigram Architects, loosely formed in 1962, is formalised as a group.
He is professor of architecture at the Bartlett School of the Built Environment, University College, University of London.
Selected buildings and projects: Arcadia (1976-78); Langen Glass Museum, Germany, (with C. Hawley, 1986); Way Out West, Berlin (1988); Housing at Lutzowplatz, Berlin (1989); Canteen block, HbK, Frankfurt (1989-92).

COOP HIMMELBLAU

WOLF PRIX

Born in 1942 in Vienna, Austria.
Studied at the University of Vienna and at SCI-Arc in Los Angeles, USA.
Teaches at the School of Applied Arts in Vienna, at SCI-Arc, at the Architectural Association in London and at Harvard University, USA.

HELMUT SWICZINSKY

Born in 1944 in Poznan, Poland.
Studied at the University of Vienna and at SCI-Arc.
1968: Coop Himmelblau founded in Vienna.

Selected buildings and projects: Reiss Bar, Vienna (1977); Rote Engel, Vienna (1981); Groningen Museum, Netherlands (1994).

DECQ AND CORNETTE

ODILE DECQ

Born in 1955 at Laval, France.
1978: Architecture diploma, Paris.
1979: Diploma of Urbanism and Urban planning, École des sciences politiques, Paris.

BENOIT CORNETTE

Born in 1953 at La Guerche de Bretagne, France.
1978: Graduated in Medicine, Rennes.
1985: Graduated in Architecture, Paris.

Selected buildings and projects: Banque populaire de l'Ouest, Rennes, France (1990); Control Tower, Bordeaux Airport (1993 competition).

DILLER & SCOFIDIO

ELISABETH DILLER

Born in 1954 in Lodz, Poland.
1979: graduated from the Cooper Union School of Architecture, New York.
Teaches at Princeton University.

RICARDO SCOFIDIO

Born in 1935 in New York, USA.
1960: graduated in Architecture from the Columbia University, New York.
Teaches at the Cooper Union School of Architecture, New York.

Buildings and projects: Para-Site, video installation, New York (1991); SuitCase Studies, installation, New York (1992); Permanent "marquee" for largest movie theatre in the world, San José, California (1995).

GÜNTHER DOMENIG

Born in 1934 in Klagenfurt, Germany.
International Urbanism and Architecture prize, Cannes (1969); European prize for building in metal (1975).
Professor, University of Technology, Graz, Austria.
Selected buildings and projects: swimming pool and restaurant, Olympic Games, Munich (1975); Savings Bank, Vienna (1979); Stone House, Steindorf (1986); Power Station, Unzmarkt (1988); RESOWI, Graz University (1994-96).

DU BESSET AND LYON

PIERRE DU BESSET

Born in 1949 in Paris, France.
1974: Diploma from the École des Beaux-Arts, Paris.
1977-85: worked with Jean Nouvel.

DOMINIQUE LYON

Born in 1954 in Paris, France.
1979: Diploma from the École des Beaux-Arts, Paris.
1979-85: worked with Jean Nouvel, then with Frank O. Gehry.
1986: creation of Du Besset and Lyon.

Selected buildings and projects: maison de La Villette, parc de La Villette, Paris, (1987); offices for *Le Monde* newspaper, Paris (1990); French pavilion at Expo'92, Seville, (competition entry 1992); University Library at Jussieu, Paris, (competition entry 1992).

SIR NORMAN FOSTER

Born in 1935 in Manchester, Great Britain.
1961: BA in architecture and city planning from Manchester University.
1962: M.Arch. from Yale University, USA.
1967: creation of Foster Associates, now Sir Norman Foster & Partners.
Knighted by H.M. the Queen in 1990; Gold Medal, American Institute of Architects, 1994.
Selected buildings and projects: Sainsbury Centre for the Visual Arts, East Anglia, Great Britain (1974-78); Hong Kong & Shanghai Bank, Hong Kong (1979); Sackler Galleries at the Royal Academy of Arts, London (1979); Stansted international airport (1991); Commerzbank headquarters, Frankfurt (1991); Chek Lap Kok Airport, Hong Kong (1992); Nîmes Arts Centre (1993).

MASSIMILIANO FUKSAS

Born in 1944 in Rome, Italy.
1967: set up his practice in Rome.
1969: Architecture diploma from La Sapienza University, Rome.
Has taught at the University of La Sapienza in Rome, at the Fine Arts Academy in Stuttgart, at the École spéciale d'architecture, Paris and at Columbia University, New York.
Selected buildings and projects: Paliano Gymnasium, Italy (1985); Orvieto Cemetery, Italy (1990); restructuring of the banks of the Seine at Clichy, France (winning competition entry, 1991); the old harbour in Hamburg, Germany (winning competition entry, 1991); mediatheque, Rezé, France (1991).

FRANK O. GEHRY

Born in 1929 in Toronto, Canada.
1954: architecture diploma from the University of Southern California, USA.
1960: town planning diploma from Harvard University, USA
Worked with Victor Gruen, Pereira & Luckman in Los Angeles, and with André Rémondet in Paris.
1962: founded Frank O. Gehry & Associates.
Pritzker Prize (1989); Lilian Gish prize (1994).
Selected buildings and projects: studio for Ron Davis, Malibu (1972); Gehry's house additions, Santa Monica (1978); Loyola Law School, Los Angeles (1982); Winton House, Minneapolis (1987); Vitra Museum, Weil am Rhein (1989); Eurodisney Leisure Centre, France (1990); concert hall, Los Angeles (winning competition entry, 1991); American Center, Paris (1993).

NICHOLAS GRIMSHAW

Born in 1939 in Hove, Great Britain.
1965: Architectural Association Diploma, London.
1980: founded Nicholas Grimshaw & Partners.
Fellow of the Chartered Society of Designers (1988); Hon. Doctorate of Letters from the University of the South Bank, London (1993); C.B.E. (1993); Mies Van der Rohe Pavilion prize (1995).
Selected buildings and projects: Oxford Ice Rink (1982); Financial Times printing works, London (1988); Combined Operations Centre for British Airways, Heathrow (1993); British Pavilion at Expo'92, Seville (1992).

ZAHA HADID

Born in 1950 in Bagdad, Iraq.
1977: Architectural Association Diploma, London.
Has taught at the Architectural Association, Columbia University, Harvard University and the University of Graz in Austria.
Architectural Design Gold Medal, London (1982).
Selected buildings and projects: The Peak, Hong Kong (winning competition entry 1983); Video Pavilion, Groningen, Netherlands (1990); Mansoon Restaurant, Sapporo, Japan (1990).

ITSUKO HASEGAWA

Born in 1941 in Shizuoka, Japan.
1964: graduated from the department of architecture, Kanto Gakuin University, Japan.
1964-69: worked with Kiyonori Kikutake.
1969-78: assistant to Kazuo Shinohara at the Institute of Technology, Tokyo.
1979: established Itsuko Hasegawa Atelier.
Japan Architecture Institute Prize (1986); Aron Arts prize (1990).

Teaches at Tokyo Denki University and at Harvard University, USA.
Selected buildings and projects: Atelier at Tomigaya, Japan (1986); Shiranui Hospital, Japan (1990); Cona Village, Japan (1990); Footwork Computer Centre, Japan (1992).

JACQUES HONDELATTE

Born in 1942 at L'Absie, France.
1967: founded Duprat, Fagart, Hondelatte.
1969: Architecture Diploma from the École d'architecture, Bordeaux.
1978: established his own practice in Bordeaux.
Teaches at the École d'architecture, Bordeaux.
Selected buildings and projects: council housing, Castres, France (1979); housing, Angoulême, France (1983); school at Pessac, France (with Jean Nouvel, competition entry, 1984); University library, Jussieu, France, (competition entry,1992); Lalanne building, Messanges, France (1995).

FRANKLIN D. ISRAEL

Born in 1945, New York, USA. Died June 1996.
1967: BA from the University of Pennsylvania.
1968: Yale University.
1971: MA from Columbia University, New York.
1975-77: senior architect at Llewelyn Davies.
1977: established Franklin D. Israel Design Associates.
Rome Prize in architecture (1973).
Professor at the School of Art and Architecture at the University of California at Los Angeles.
Selected buildings and projects: corporate headquarters for Limelight Productions, Hollywood (1991) and Virgin Records, Beverly Hills (1991); Dan House, Malibu (1995).

TOYO ITO

Born in 1941 in Seoul, Korea.
1965: architecture diploma from the University of Tokyo.
1971: establishment of Urban Robot (URBOT), Tokyo, now Toyo Ito & Associates Architects.
Mainichi Art Prize for the Yatsushiro Municipal Museum, Japan (1992).
Selected buildings and projects: Yatsushiro Municipal Museum, Kumamoto (1991); Shimosuwa Municipal Museum, Nagano (1993); Aged People's Home in Yatsushiro, Kumamoto (1994); Yatsushiro Fire Station, Kumamoto (1995).

DANIEL LIBESKIND

Born in 1945 in Lodz, Poland.
1970: architecture diploma from the Cooper Union School of Architecture, New York.
1972: postgraduate course in the history and theory of architecture, University of Essex, Great Britain.
Head of the Department of Architecture at the Cranbrook Academy of Art
Selected buildings and projects: Yatai Pavilion World Design Exhibition, Japan (1989); "Symbol for the City", urban design construction, Groningen, Netherlands (1993).

ENRIC MIRALLES MOYA

Born in 1955 in Spain.
1978: diploma in architecture from ETSAB, Barcelona.
1984: establishment of the Miralles and Carme Pinós practice, now Enric Miralles Moya.
Teaches at ETSAB, Barcelona and has an architecture Master Class at the Städelschule in Frankfurt.
Selected buildings and projects: Social Centre

for Circulo de Lectores, Madrid (1992); La Mina Civic Centre, Barcelona (1993); Ramblas in Reus, Tarragona (1993); National Rhythmic Gymnastics Centre, Alicante (1994).

MORPHOSIS

THOM MAYNE

Born in 1944, at Waterbury, Connecticut, USA.
1968: BA in architecture from the University of Southern California.
1978: MA in architecture from Harvard University.
1972: Co-founder of the Southern Californian Institute of Architecture (SCI-Arc).
1975: establishment of Morphosis with Michael Rotondi.
Teaches at Harvard, Yale and SCI-Arc.
Rome Prize (1977); architecture prize of the American Academy of Arts and Letters (1992).

Selected buildings and projects: Cedars Sinai Comprehensive Cancer Centre, Los Angeles (1987); AGB Library, Berlin (1988); MTV Studios, Potsdamer Platz, Berlin (1990).

ERIC OWEN MOSS

Born in 1943 in Los Angeles, USA.
1965: BA from the University of California at Los Angeles (UCLA)
1968: MA from the University of Berkeley.
1974: architecture diploma from Harvard University.
1974: establishment of Eric Owen Moss Architects.
Teaches at the Southern California Institute of Architecture (SCI-Arc).
Selected buildings and projects: Lindblade Tower, Culver City (1989); the Lawson/Western House, Los Angeles (1993); Ince Theatre, Culver City (1994).

JEAN NOUVEL

Born in 1945 in Fumel, France.
1970: establishment of his first office, now called Architectures Jean Nouvel
1972: Diploma of the École des Beaux-Arts, Paris.
Chevalier of the Order of Arts and Letters (1983); chevalier of the Order of Merit (1987); Architecture Grand Prix (1987).
Selected buildings and projects: Institute of the Arab World, Paris, with G. Lezenes, P. Soria, Architecture Studio (1987); Agence CLMBBDO, île Saint-Germain (1993); Conference Centre, Tours (1993); social housing, Bezons (1993).

OFFICE OF METROPOLITAN ARCHITECTURE

REM KOOLHAAS

Born in 1944 in Rotterdam, Netherlands.
1972: Architectural Association Diploma, London.
1974: establishment of OMA in London and New York with Madelon Vriesendorp, and Zoe and Elia Zenghelis.
1978: publication of «Delirious New York».
1980: establishment of OMA in Rotterdam.
Selected buildings and projects: Dance Theatre, The Hague (1987); Byzantium, Amsterdam (1990); Nexus housing, Fukuoka (1991); Konsthal, Rotterdam (1992); Lille Grand Palais, Lille, France (1994).

RENZO PIANO

Born in 1937 in Genoa, Italy.
1964: diploma from Milan Polytechnic.
1965-70: worked with Louis Kahn in Philadelphia and Z.S. Malowski in London.

1971-80: collaboration with Richard Rogers, Peter Rice and Richard Fitzgerald.
1981: establishment of Building Workshop in Genoa and Paris.
Selected buildings and projects: Pompidou Centre, Paris (1977); De Ménil Foundation, Houston, Texas (1989); *Crown Princess* liner (1989); Bercy commercial centre, Paris (1990).

CHRISTIAN DE PORTZAMPARC

Born in 1944 in Brittany, France.
1969: Diploma from the École des Beaux-Arts, Paris.
1971: established his own practice.
Taught at the École spéciale d'architecture, Paris and at the Paris-Nanterre Architecture School.
Commander of the Order of Arts and Letters; Architecture Grand Prix (1992); Pritzker Prize (1994).
Selected buildings and projects: Les Hautes Formes housing, Paris (1975); Opera Dance Academy, Nanterre (1983), Bourdelle Museum, Paris (1992).

FRANÇOIS ROCHE

Born in 1961 in Paris, France.
1987: Architecture Diploma.
1993: demonstration at the Institut français d'architecture.
Villa des Médicis external fellowship.
Selected buildings and projects: House of Japan, Paris (competition entry 1990); film storage building, Bois d'Arcy (1991); Art and Media Museum (competition entry, 1991); Spreebogen, Berlin (competition entry, 1993); renovation of the Deligny swimming pool, Paris (1993).

SIR RICHARD ROGERS

Born in 1933 in Florence, Italy.
1959: Architectural Association Diploma, London.
1961: Architecture Diploma from Yale University, USA.
1963: establishment of Team 4 with Sue Rogers and Norman and Wendy Foster.
1971: establishment of Piano & Rogers, now Sir Richard Rogers & Partners in London and Tokyo.
Légion d'honneur (1986); Royal Gold Medal for Architecture (London, 1985); knighted by H.M. the Queen in 1991; Chevalier of the Order of Arts and Letters (1995).
Taught at the Universities of California, Princeton, Harvard and Berkeley.
Selected buildings and projects: Pompidou Centre, Paris (1977); Lloyds Building,

London (1986); INMOS factory, Newport, Great Britain (1982); headquarters building for Channel 4 television, London (1991).

SHIN TAKAMATSU

Born in 1948 in Shimana, Japan.
1971: graduated in architecture from Kyoto University.
1974: MA in architecture from Kyoto University.
1980: doctorate from Kyoto University.
Establishment of Shin Takamatsu Architects & Associates in Kyoto.
1992: established Takamatsu & Lahyani Architects in Berlin
Fuchi Bikan Prize (1983); International Interior Design prize (1987); Grand Prix of the Osaka Architects' Association (1987).
Selected buildings and projects: Wako Building, Tokyo (1990); Sand Museum, Nima (1990); Syntax, Kyoto (1990); Solaris Building, Awagasa (1990); Earthtecture, Tokyo, (1991).

MASAHARU TAKASAKI

Born in 1953, in Kagoshima, Japan.
1976: graduated from the Meijo University School of Architecture.
1982: founded Takasaki Manobito Institute.
1990: founded Masaharu Takasaki Architects.
First prize in *The Japan Architect* International House Design Competition.
Teaches at Stuttgart Technological University and the University of Graz.
Selected buildings and projects: Crystal Light, Tokyo (1987); Tamana City Observatory Museum, Kumamoto (1992); Kuju National Park Restaurant, Oita (1994); Kihoku-cho Astronomical Museum, Kagoshima (1995); Shomyo Kindergarten, Kagoshima (1995).

KIYOSHI SEY TAKEYAMA

Born in 1954 in Osaka, Japan.
1977: graduated from Kyoto University School of Architecture.
1979: graduated from Tokyo University Graduate School of Architecture.
Associate Professor at Kyoto University School of Architecture
Selected buildings and projects: OXY Nogizaka, Tokyo (1987); D-Hôtel, Osaka (1989); house in Modorigaoka, Tokyo (1989); TERRAZA, Tokyo (1991); Blue Screen House, Osaka (1993).

BERNARD TSCHUMI

Born in 1944 in Lausanne, Switzerland.
1969: degree in architecture from the Federal Institute of Technology (ETH), Zurich.

Dean of Columbia University Graduate School of Architecture.
Selected buildings and projects: Chief Architect for the Parc de La Villette project, Paris (1983); city-bridges, Lausanne (1988); video gallery, Groningen, Netherlands (1989); Chartres master plan, France (winning competition entry, 1991).

LEBBEUS WOODS

Born in 1940 in Lansing, Michigan, USA.
Graduated from Purdue University School of Engineering and the University of Illinois School of Architecture.
Has been Visiting Professor at SCI-Arc, Harvard and Columbia Universities; and is now Visiting Professor of Architecture at the Cooper Union School of Architecture, New York, and at the University of Innsbruck, Austria.
Selected buildings and projects: Zagreb-Free-Zone (1991); War and Architecture (1992-93); apartment blocks Electroprivrede Building, Unis Towers, Sarajevo (1994); Havana Projects (1995).

SHOEI YOH

Born in 1940 in Kumamoto, Japan.
1962: graduated in economics from Keio Gijuku University, Tokyo.
1964: foreign student grant in aid, majored in Fine and Applied Arts at Wittenberg University, Springfield, Ohio, USA.
1970: Shoei Yoh & Associates Fukuoka.
Visiting Professor at Columbia University Graduate School of Architecture, New York and lecturer at Kyushi University, Japan.
Japan Institute of Architecture Prize (1983 and 1989); IAKS prize Cologne, gold medal (1993).
Selected buildings and projects: stainless steel house with light grille (1981); glass house between sea and sky (1991); Galaxie, Toyama and gymnasium (1992); community centre and kindergarten, Naiju (1994); centre for children and old people (1995).

GLOSSARY

ARCHITECTS

Alberti Leon Battista (1404-72)
Painter, musician, scientist, architect, Alberti is a Renaissance man. His treatise «De re aedificatoria» defines a building as a whole where all the parts are in harmony, and architecture as an autonomous discipline.

Baumgarten Paul
Modernist Berlin architect who carried out interesting research during the thirties with Eternit. He built the station at Müllverlade on the Spree Canal (1950) and an elegant building in the Hansaviertel district (1957).
His restructuring of the Reichstag during the sixties is being destroyed to make way for Sir Norman Foster's new project.

Bayer Herbert
Bayer was born in Austria at the beginning of the century and was a pupil of the Bauhaus at Weimar before becoming a teacher of typography and advertizing at Dessau. After 1938 he continued his career in the United States.

Behrens Peter (1868-1940)
Heir to Schinkel and the classical tradition, Behrens is also the architect who, at the beginning of the century, instituted new relations with industry. His collaboration with A.E.G. led to the advent of industrial design. Three young architects worked in his office around 1910: Walter Gropius, Le Corbusier and Mies Van der Rohe.

Gropius Walter (1883-1969)
Influenced by Behrens and industrial rationalism, Gropius established the Bauhaus teaching, and then went into exile, first in England, then in the United States where he was very influential through his teaching at Harvard. He advised Emery Roth & Sons on the Pan Am Building in New York (1964).

Hejduk John (1929-)
This American architect and poet was among the first to introduce fiction into architectural thinking. His influence springs from his role as head of the Cooper Union School of Architecture (since 1964) and as theoretician and member of the New York Five (with Peter Eisenman, Michael Graves, Charles Gwathmey and Richard Meier).

Isozaki Arata (1931-)
A disciple of Kenzo Tange, and member of the Metabolist Movement, steeped in western culture (Duchamp and Marilyn Monroe), Isozaki's oeuvre is both brilliant and eclectic.

Johnson Philip (1906-)
First curator of the department of architecture at the Museum of Modern Art in New York, Johnson became an architect in 1940. After facilitating the exile of Mies Van der Rohe in the United States in 1938 he was his most assiduous pupil until he embraced post-modernism of which he became the most cynical promoter.

Kahn Louis I. (1901-1975)
Educated in Philadelphia, Kahn received late recognition for his building for the Yale Gallery (1954) before becoming the archetypal modern with buildings such as the Salk Institute, La Jolla (1965), the Kimbell Museum, Dallas and the Dacca Parliament in Bangladesh (1974).

Kikutake Kiyonori (1928-)
Creator and leader of the Japanese Metabolists, Kikutake's work consists of large utopian projects and megastructures, aerial and underwater cities of a kind that proliferated in Japan in the sixties.

Kleihues Josef Paul (1933-)
German architect whose work melds Italian rationalism with Prussian classicism. From 1979 on he was the influential director of the International Building Exhibition (IBA) in Berlin.

Laprade Albert
French architect who, with L. Bazin, built the Marbeuf Garage (1929) – now destroyed – and played an active role in the 1937 Paris Exposition.

Le Corbusier Charles Edouard Jeanneret called (1887-1966)
One of the great figures of the twentieth century whose theoretical work leading to certain questionable architectural and urban principles sometimes camouflages an oeuvre that is both innovative and infinitely variable. His masterpieces: the Villas Savoye at Poissy and Stein at Garches, the Salvation Army Hostel, Paris, the Unité d'habitation in Marseille, the monastery of la Tourette, the chapel at Ronchamp, and Chandigarh in India are among the most important works of this century.

Lissitzky El (1890-1941)
A founder member and proselyte of Russian Constructivism in the twenties.
His « Proun », indebted to Malevich and Suprematism, advocated a new state of art between painting and architecture.

Loos Adolf (1870-1933)
Viennese but fiercely opposed to the Secession, Loos travelled in America where he discovered Sullivan and the Chicago school which inspired his famous polemical essay "Ornament and Crime." The Steiner House in Vienna (1910) is the first concrete house. His rigorously classical buildings have an elegant refinement.

Meier Richard (1934-)
The American architect Richard Meier has perfected the architecture of Le Corbusier's «white villas».

Mendelsohn Eric (1887-1953)
German Expressionnist and architect of a cult building of its time: the Einstein Tower in Potsdam (1924). Mendelsohn built some of the most remarkable commercial buildings (shops and offices) in Germany during the thirties. From 1933 he pursued his career in England and then in the United States.

Mies Van der Rohe Ludwig (1886-1969)
One of the great masters of twentieth-century architecture, the most classical and the most influential of the «pure» modernists. His master-pieces include: the Barcelona pavilion (1927), the apartment blocks on Lake Shore Drive, Chicago (1951), the Seagram Building, New York (1958) and the Berlin National Gallery (1968).

Mozuna Kiko (1941-)
Japanese architect who reconciles the traditions of east and west in strongly symbolic objects.

Neutra Richard (1892-1970)
Viennese architect in exile in the United States where he practised in Chicago before settling in Los Angeles. He built the Lovell House there in 1929. It remains one of the models of modern heroic architecture. He greatly influenced a whole generation of young Californian architects.

Piñon & Viaplana
Architects belonging to the new Barcelona School.

Piños Carmen
Spanish architect, partner of Enric Miralles Moya.

Poelzig Hans (1869-1936)
German Expressionist architect influential during the twenties (Grosses Schauspielhaus, Berlin, 1919). His work was discredited by the rationalists, but is now once again attracting interest.

Price Cedric
British architect, dandy and eminence grise for a whole generation, Price brilliantly synthesizes high tech, ecology and recycling in his theoretical projects (Potteries Thinkbelt, Fun Palace) and his temporary installations. A key work is the InterAction Centre, London (1977). Teaches at the Architectural Association.

Scharoun Hans (1893-1972)
One of the first Expressionists, member of Bruno Taut's «glass chain», Hans Scharoun was Chief Architect for the reconstruction of Berlin and was reponsible for the Berlin-capital plan in 1957 and some apartment blocks (Romeo & Juliet, Stuttgart). He built his master-piece, the Berlin Philharmonic Hall, in 1964.

Schinkel Karl Friedrich (1781-1841)
The purest of the Berlin classicists, Schinkel influenced both Peter Behrens and Mies Van der Rohe.

Schindler Rudolf (1887-1953)
Viennese architect, an admirer of Adolf Loos, Schindler emigrated to the United States in the second decade of the century and worked with Frank Lloyd Wright before setting up his own practice in Los Angeles. He had a brilliant but uneven career leaving two undisputed masterpieces: his own house in King's Road and Dr. Lovell's Beach House at Newport (1926). He was influenced by De Stijl. His subtle sensitivity to the Southern Californian setting and the appropriateness of his buildings to that environment is increasingly appreciated today.

Shinohara Kazuo (1925-)
Japanese architect of very elegant houses in Japanese style that are subtly symbolic. But his later works are vidently high tech and express the chaos inherent in the Japanese city.

Stirling Sir James (1926-1992)
First recognized as an orthodox modernist, Stirling was influenced by the historicists and at the end of his career built curious structures in which Egyptian, classical and baroque play an

ironic role. The Staatsgalerie in Stuttgart is his masterpiece.

Taut Bruno (1880-1938)
His Glass Pavilion at the Werkbund exhibition in Cologne (1914) was the prelude to the Glass Architecture which he developed with the Expressionists of the Novembergruppe. He built two remarkable «Siedlungen» in Berlin: the Britz complex (with Martin Wagner, 1930) and «Uncle Tom's Cabin» (1931). He left Germany in 1933, going first to Japan and then to Turkey.

Tusquets Oscar (1941-)
A Barcelona architect who puts the anecdotal above theory, the particular above the general, ambiguity above clarity and the figurative aove the abstract. He is closest to Venturi of all the Europeans.

Van Doesburg Theo (1883-1931)
Painter and founder (with J.J. Oud) of the De Stijl movement that applies Mondrian's ideas to architecture and to design. He was their most energetic promoter. His only buildings are a café in Strasbourg, l'Aubette (with Jean Arp), and his own studio/house at Meudon.

Venturi Robert
American architect whose two books «Complexity and contradiction in architecture» and «Learning from Las Vegas» have made him the most influential theoretician of the Post-Modern movement.

Webb Michael (1937-)
British architect, member of Archigram.

Wright Frank Lloyd (1867-1959)
The great master of American architecture whose career covers a large part of the twentieth century. It began in Chicago with Sullivan, continued in Japan, then in the United States. Wright built more than four hundred buildings including: the Unity Temple, Oak Park (1906), Frederick C. Robie House (1909), the Miniaturan, Pasadena, Fallingwater (1936), Johnson's Wax Company Administration Building (1936), the Luckland Campus, and the Solomon R. Guggenheim Museum (1956).

BUILDINGS

Broadacre City
Frank Lloyd Wright's plan for a democratic city with no hierarcy and no city centre.

Crystal Palace
Built for the 1851 Great Exhibition in London, the Crystal Palace was an immediate success because of its size, its audacity and its prefabricated iron and glass structure. It was taken down at the end of the Exhibition and erected again in Sydenham but was destroyed by fire in 1936.

Garden City
Inspired by the socialist Utopians of the nineteenth century, Ebenezer Howard's garden cities reconcile the city-dweller with nature and create a self-sufficient community life away from the turpitude of the city. The first one was Letchworth (1903).

Glass Pavilion
Built in 1914 for the Deutscher Werkbund exhibition, Bruno Taut's Glass Pavilion is an example of a Modern architecture whose constructional rigour does not exclude formal preoccupations.

National Gallery, Berlin
The last building by Mies Van der Rohe (1968). The architecture of this large-scale pavilion lies somewhere between Prussian classicism and Japanese minimalism.

Pompidou Centre
The most extreme example of a high-tech monument, the architects of which - Piano and Rogers - have stressed its artisanal charcter on innumerable occasions.

Radiant City
The ideal city according to Le Corbusier (1935).

Ronchamp
The most convoluted of Le Corbusier's works, built towards the end of his career at the same time as he wrote the poem to the right angle.

Siedlungen
Between the wars Germany produced a series of apartment blocks inspired by Modern architects. The growth of social housing was spectacular and often of very good quality for the time. May in Frankfurt, Gropius, Taut, Scharoun, and Mies Van der Rohe in Berlin were among those who contributed to this development.

GROUPS

Archigram
The first issue of *Archigram* was published in 1961. It was a kind of magazine put together by a group of young London architects (Warren Chalk, Peter Cook, Denis Crompton, David Greene, Ron Herron, Michael Webb). Eight issues were published in which the group developed an architecture inspired by the consumer society and Pop images and which, once rationalized, would constitute the basis for British high-tech.

Graz, School of
In the sixties, Raimund Abram and Günther Domenig founded a movement in violent reaction to the International Style. It continued in the seventies with such young architects as Enfried Huth, Szyskowitz & Kowalsky, Klaus Kada and Gerngross & Richter. The monument to this period is the refectory of the Ursuline nuns at Graz, a zoomorphic building in concrete, designed by Domenig and Huth (1976).

Haus Rücker Co
Founded in Vienna at the beginning of the seventies by Laurids Ortner, Günther Zamp and Klaus Pinter, Haus Rücker Co has organized various demonstrations that question our use of the city and the introduction of communications technologies into the urban environment.

Independent Group
Formed in London in 1952, the I.G. included artists Richard Hamilton and Eduardo Paolozzi, critics Reyner Banham and Lawrence Alloway and architects Peter and Alison Smithson. The «Parallel of Life and Art» exhibition at the Institute of Contemporary Art in 1953, punctuated with advertisements, popular magazines and science fiction images prefigures Pop Art and the more romantic side of high-tech architecture.

Missing Link Productions
Space capsules and inflatable structures constitute the weapons of this Viennese group of the seventies for the transformation of the city. Later, Missing Link came back to earth to study the Viennese Siedlungen of the thirties from a historicist rather than futurist viewpoint.

Novembergruppe
For a short period from 1918 to 1920, the Novembergruppe comprised all the young architectural activists in Berlin, from Gropius to Mendelsohn and from Taut to Mies Van der Rohe in an expressionist movement. The group was dissolved following the repression of the Spartakist revolt. Bruno Taut continued its Expressionist vein in his «chain of glass», while Gropius went on to found the Bauhaus.

ENGINEERS

Arup Ove (1895-1993)
A Scandinavian who emigrated to London, Ove Arup played a role in almost every great adventure in contemporary architecture and collaborated with architects as diverse as Lubetkin, the Smithsons, Jorn Utzon and Piano & Rogers.

Brunel Isambard Kingdom (1806-1859)
One of the great British engineers of the nineteenth century. His structures include the Clifton Suspension Bridge at Bristol and the liners *Great Western* and *Great Eastern*. He was also the inventor of the first portable hospital designed for the Crimean War.

Candela Felix (1910-1994)
A Spaniard who emigrated to Mexico, Candela specialised in curtains of thin concrete (Church of Our Lady of the Miracles in Mexico, 1955).

Fitzpatrick Antony (1955-)
A British engineer, part of the brilliant Ove Arup team. Has worked with leading international architects including Sir Norman Foster (the Hong Kong & Shanghai Bank).

Freyssinet Eugène (1879-1962)
A French engineer who designed bridges and the magnificent hangar at Orly Airport (1916).

Fuller Richard Buckminster (1895-1989)
The self-taught Fuller was one of the most brilliant engineers of the twentieth century. Inspired by car production, he designed an industrialised house, the Dymaxion in 1927. Later his research was concerned with reticular structures which led to the invention of the geodesic dome.

Morandi Riccardo (1902-)
An Italian engineer famous for his structures in prestressed concrete: the Arno bridge (1956), the Polcevera viaduct (1965) and the A6 motorway in France.

Nervi Pier Luigi (1891-1979)
Italian engineer who developed a technique called ferrocemento in which a series of steel meshes make concrete more tensile. His major work is the Turin Exhibition Hall (1949).

Paxton Joseph (1803-1865)
A British gardener, Paxton was self-taught and built innovative glasshouses before his masterpiece, the Crystal Palace, in 1851.

Prouvé Jean (1901-1984)
This French engineer perfected the curtain wall: from the Maison du Peuple in Clichy (with Beaudoin and Lods, 1939) to the first tower at La Défense in Paris, and from his metal house in Meudon to his basic housing for the Abbé Pierre, his work is the fruit of a stubborn and generous perfectionism.

Rice Peter (1935-1992)
A senior engineer at Ove Arup, Peter Rice's career was both brilliant and tumultuous: he was the structural engineer for the Sydney Opera House and for the Pompidou Centre. Renzo Piano has said of him that he solved technical problems like a virtuoso pianist playing with his eyes closed.

INSTITUTIONS

Deutscher Werkbund
Founded in 1907 by Muthesius to bring about a fusion of the arts, architecture and the applied arts, the Werkbund was responsible for three important exhibitions: Cologne in 1914 which brought together the pioneers of the alliance of the arts and industry including Van de Velde, Gropius, Behrens, Hoffman and Taut; Weissenhof in 1927, a development built by the best European architects of the time; and the 1930 Paris exposition which revealed, through Gropius, the work of Herbert Bayer, Moholy Nagy and Breuer, all refugees from the Bauhaus.

I.A.U.S (Institute of Architecture and Urban Studies)
The Institute of Architecture and Urban Studies was founded in New York by Peter Eisenman. It acts as a theoretical laboratory and exhibition space.

I.B.A.
The Internationale Bauaustellung (international building exhibition) follows in the footsteps of Weissenhof (an exhibition held in Stuttgart in 1927 that presented models of contemporary housing). In the course of reconstruction work on the city, a first exhibition on the theme of housing was held in Berlin, leading to the building of the Hansaviertel district in 1957, on which an impressive number of talented European architects worked. The success of this operation led to the institutionalization of the I.B.A.

Architecture Schools mentioned in the text

Architectural Association, London;
School of Architecture and Conservation, Columbia University, New York, USA;
Cooper Union School of Architecture, New York;
École des Beaux-Arts, Paris;
School of Architecture and Urbanism, Harvard University, Cambridge, Mass., USA;
Illinois Institue of Technology (IIT), University of Chicago, Ill., USA;
Istituto Politécnico, Milan, Italy;
Southern California Institute of Architecture (SCI-Arc), Los Angeles, Ca, USA ;
School of Architecture at the University of California at Los Angeles (UCLA), USA;
School of Architecture at the University of Southern California (USC), Los Angeles, USA;
School of Art and Architecture at Yale University, New Haven, Connecticut, USA.

Bauhaus (1919-1933)
Founded in Weimar by Walter Gropius, the Bauhaus remains the most famous school of the century both for its innovative teaching programme, the reputation of its faculty which included Johannes Itten, Vassily Kandinsky, Paul Klee, Moholy Nagy, Josef Albers, Marcel Breuer, Herbert Bayer - and for its troubled history. It was transferred from Weimar to Dessau in 1925. Gropius resigned in 1928 and was succeeded by Hannes Meyer, then Mies Van der Rohe. The school closed in Berlin in 1933 but the teaching of the Bauhaus was continued in the United States by Gropius at Harvard and Moholy Nagy at Chicago.

Hochschule für Gestaltung, Ulm.
Established by Max Bill in 1951, the Ulm School was intended as a continuation of the Bauhaus. It too had a troubled existence. Max Bill resigned in 1956 and was succeeded by Herbert Ohl. Teaching emphasised strict methodology but was gradually radicalised under the influence of Maldonado, Schnaidt and Bonsiepe and had to close down in 1968. The Ulm school remains synonymous with «Gute Form».

Vkhutemas
The Vkhutemas were created in 1918 in Moscow to combine the teaching of the arts, the applied arts and architecture. Directed by the constructivists Ladovsky, Tatlin, Rodchenko and others, who greatly influenced Soviet architecture of the twenties and were at the origin of the Bauhaus.

PHOTO CREDITS

Cover and pages 188, 190, 191, 192, 193, 194, 196, 197: photos Philippe Ruault.
Pages 2, 162, 164, 165: photos Mitsumasa Fujitsuaka.
Page 6: photo André Morain.
Page 8: photo Matsumoto Norihiko.
Page 9: photo Rivière, musée d'Orsay.
Page 10: photo CNACGP.
Page 11 right: photo Barch-Reisinger Museum, Harvard University ; left: document 1937 Exposition.
Pages 14, 16, 17, 18, 19: documents P. Cook / Ch. Hawley.
Pages 20, 22, 23, 24, 25: documents Arakawa and Madeline Gins.
Pages 26, 31, 33 bottom: photos Udo Hesse.
Page 29: city of Cologne.
Page 30: Art Institute of Chicago.
Page 33 top: photo Elisabeth Govan.
Pages 12, 34, 37, 38, 39: documents Bernard Tschumi Architects.
Page 38 top: photo Dan Cornish.
Pages 40, 42, 43: documents Lebbeus Woods.
Pages 44, 46, 47: documents François Roche.
Pages 48, 60: photos Xavier Basiana Vers.
Page 50 bottom: photo Kanji Hiwatashi.
Page 52 left: Yutaka Kinumaki.
Page 52 right: Toshimaru Kitajima.
Page 53: photo Yutaka Kinumaki.
Pages 54-55: photos Yoshio Hata.

Pages 56-57: documents Nicholas Grimshaw and Partners.
Pages 58-59: photos John Edward Linden.
Page 63: photo Richard Davies.
Page 64: document Alsop / Störmer.
Pages 66-67: photo P. Raffery.
Pages 68, 70, 71: documents Jacques Hondelatte.
Pages 72, 136, 137: photos Joshua White.
Page 74: photo Fujita.
Pages 75, 76, 77, 78: photos Nicolas Borel.
Page 79: infographics J.C. Chaulet.
Pages 80, 83: documents Agence Takeyama.
Pages 85, 86, 87: photo Satoshi Asakawa.
Page 88: photo Kozlowski.
Pages 90, 91: photos Aki Furudate.
Page 92: infographics Christophe Valtin.
Pages 94, 95: documents Decq / Cornette.
Pages 96, 98, 99: photo Gert von Bassewitz.
Pages 100, 102, 103, 104, 105: documents OMA.
Pages 106, 108, 110, 111: documents Zaha Hadid
Page 109: photos Richard Bryant
Pages 112, 116, 117, 118, 119: photos Margherita Spiluttini.
Pages 114, 115, 130, 131: photos Tom Bonner.
Pages 120, 122, 123: photos Hisao Suzuki.
Pages 124, 125: photos Christopher Yates.

Pages 126, 127: photos Grant Mudford.
Pages 128, 129: photos Paul Groh.
Pages 132, 134, 135: photos Don F. Wong.
Page 138: photo Takashi Miyamoto.
Pages 140, 144 bottom, 145 bottom: documents Emilio Ambasz.
Pages 143, 144 top, 145 top: photos Ryuzo Masunaga.
Pages 146, 149: photos Eui-Sung Vi.
Pages 147, 148: documents Morphosis.
Pages 150, 151: documents Takasaki.
Pages 152, 155, 157, 159: photos Eamonn O'Mahony.
Page 160: photo Itsuko Hasegawa.
Page 163: photo Katsuaki Furudate.
Pages 166, 167: photos Shuji Yamada.
Pages 168, 198: documents Nacasa and Partners.
Pages 170, 172, 173: documents Asymptote Architecture.
Pages 174, 175, 176, 177: documents Diller / Scofidio.
Pages 178-179: documents Du Besset and Lyon.
Pages 180-181: photos Denance Archipress.
Pages 182, 184, 185: documents Toyo Ito.
Pages 186, 187: photos Shinkendiku-Sho
Page 201: photo Retoria.

Printed in France by Groupe Horizon
Parc d'activités de la plaine de Jouques - 200, avenue de Coulin - 13420 Gémenos
Printer N° 0411-013